A Diamond in the Rough

by Lakesha Nicole Baker

Edited by DNS Media Group Inc., dnsmediagroup@yahoo.com

Be encouraged, motivated, inspired and blessed!!

Lakesha Baker

THANK YOUS

I am grateful to all who entered my life's journey and had higher hopes for me than I had for myself. There were many who were able to see me in a light when I was in the dark. Who had faith enough to walk with me. I very much appreciate, respect and remember all that you are and have been to me.

God doesn't give you the people you want; he gives you the people you need. To help you, to hurt you, to leave you, to love you and to make you the person you were meant to be. – Unknown

First and foremost, I thank God, for stepping in to protect me when I was not able to protect myself. For overlooking the disgruntled messages written in my journals meant just for HIM. Providing a way when I thought there was no way. For answering all of my prayers in a timely matter when it was most needed. Finally, for being my strength and guidance on my weakest, fogged-filled days. You are my rock and I pray that the man who presents himself in my life has the qualities of you, my FATHER.

My grandmother, Mrs. Rosa L. Baker for your sacrifices. For rescuing and caring for me as best you knew how. Finally, for being a motivator in my life and shaping me into the strong, determined woman I am today.

Ms. Cheryl Roach, for caring and accepting me into her loving family. Through the years, the love has never wavered. I admire your strength and dedication and for being the "Big Momma" in the family.

Mrs. Tracey Robinson for always loving and caring for me as your own while mommy was alive and consistently after. We've lost contact at times but distance never swayed your love and for that I'm grateful for you.

Ms. Shenetta Scott, for consistently showing concern, love and, without knowing it, filling a position in my life that was necessary.

My work world: To my supervisors for your faith in me, support and coaching: Lenia Chaves, Frances Bordoni, Ann Margaret McAdams, Dr. Linda Tewksbury, Deborah and Warren Fulwood, Winston, Theresa Ruggeri, Ruth and Bernice

BIO

My name is Lakesha Nicole Baker. I am a 36-year-old African-American woman. I was born in the small town of Orangeburg, South Carolina, where I lived for nine years before a horrific tragedy led to my moving to New York City to be raised by my grandmother in the Bronx.

I am the mother of a beautiful 12-year-old named Kayla Eunice Jones. Her existence has given me a greater sense of emotional and mental strength and stability.

Indeed, a gift and a better extension of me, Kayla's existence has allowed me to revisit and vicariously live my childhood over through her. The good, bad and indifferent has shaped me into being a better person and mother to an amazing blessing sent by my Heavenly Father in my greatest time of need.

Despite many trials, tribulations and uncertainties of life, through psychological toughness, I have survived, managing to obtain a bachelor's degree in computer management and now working toward a master's in psychology. I challenge myself to learn more about my diagnoses of post-traumatic stress syndrome, while remaining competitive, fully committing myself to every activity I've been involved in, which gives me great feelings of control and sanity.

Control was something everyone else seemed to have had over me in my life for years. Hence, I truly take charge and full advantage of opportunities that come my way and make miracles happen. I have a strong determination to overcome this illness as I have the many other challenges in my life thus far.

My ultimate goal in life is to be a better me and use my experiences, backed by my education, to provide mental and moral support to another. Whether near or far, readers will hopefully be motivated and inspired by the sharing of my story. I eventually hope to become a mentor and role model. This will give me great satisfaction, and my life more meaning.

POEM

A Diamond in the Rough
Words with such powerful meaning
A Diamond in the Rough
Inspired by true strength and achievement
Every past leads to a present
Every present leads to a future
Nothing lasts forever
So all rough paths will eventually become smoother
With time there comes growth
With growth there comes change
For one to experience true joy
One must first learn to appreciate pain
A Diamond in the Rough
A true journey still in the making
A Diamond in the Rough
The true life of Lakesha Nicole Baker

DIAMOND IN THE ROUGH

An uncut diamond, the goodness or other positive qualities of which are often hidden by a harsh or unremarkable surface appearance.

Diamond was a name that was first given to me by my parents as an extension: Lakesha Nicole Baker Diamond Smith. When I saw my birth certificate and realized that Diamond Smith was not shown, I stopped using it.

But the name came about again when I started modeling in the latter part of my teenage years. Some used to say that I resembled the actress LisaRaye. I was unfamiliar with who she was, and it was around the time she starred in the movie "Players Club." I took the time to watch the movie, and to my surprise, her character's stage name was Diamond. Despite the activity for which her name came about, the message behind her overcoming all obstacles and succeeding in the goal set out was admirable.

Your current circumstance does not define you. Decisions we make play a huge role and have a significant impact in our journeys. However, when you have a plan, all things are possible.

After watching the movie, I reclaimed the name. And since then, the name has gained so much more meaning. I would often get compliments on the brightness of my smile, with a spirit that is easily recognized as genuine and a personality that sparkled. All the while I was experiencing the most darkest and troubling time in my life.

I have always been a shy, behind-the-scenes, low key, humble, private person. To have attention directed my way or to be the popular or main character of any event was not of interest. As I have grown into a more confident individual and gained a greater understanding of self, I have come to realize that the headliner role is the position for which I have been prepped.

I have finally seen that light at the end of the tunnel. I share with you my painful journey, my struggle to mentally, physically and emotionally survive even when the odds were against me. I have truly embraced who I am and where I came from and am certain my story will inspire and motivate another.

The cover photo of this book, taken by photographer Jonathan C. Ellerbee of Great Entertainment Inc., was perfect for the purpose of representing my strength from overcoming and humbleness as I reflect on what you are about to read. I felt so empowered standing in front of Greek Goddess of Wisdom and Messenger of God. Yet, for the first time saw the hurt in my eyes.

Taking it all is stride as I continue to seek my purpose and grow in wisdom.

LIFE-CHANGING TRAGEDY

"Diamond, wake up, Mommy's screaming. Imma jump out of the window and go for help," says my brother Xavier.

As I awaken, Mommy's screams are getting louder. I grabbed a teddy bear off my brother's bed and put it over my little cousin Nikkia, who was 1 year old at the time, with hopes no one would know she was under it. Then, I walked toward the sound of my mother's screams.

I pulled aside the curtains that led to the kitchen that replaced my bedroom door. I saw a man in his boxers and my mother up against the back door attempting to shield herself.

"What are you doing to my mommy?" I screamed.

A man who had been introduced to my mom weeks before was now in my kitchen. It looked like he was hitting her. Under different circumstances, I would've run to grab a weapon to help my mother. But within seconds—before I could move and realize that it was a knife in his hand and that he had been stabbing my mother—he had turned and stabbed me two inches below my heart.

Friday, May 5, 1989. It marks the unforgettable anniversary of when my life changed forever and the South would never be the same for me. We lived in a quiet neighborhood where most were family or longtime friends. We would be outside on sunny days playing hopscotch, double Dutch and freeze tag, climbing trees, going bike riding or even picking fruit off the trees.

Mommy had been up bright and early that day, ironing our clothes. This was the day she was to have graduated from nursing school—one of her biggest accomplishments after having us. A knock on the door startled her; it was only 6 a.m.

It was the man, the neighbor's grandson. My mother answered through the door without opening it, "Who is it?" He replied, "Fred." Fred was the grandson of Ms. Cunningham. He had recently come from the North, as most families did every year for the summer family reunion. Ms. Cunningham was well known in the area. She was a best friend of my great-grandma Ann. Great-grandma Ann had introduced Fred to my mother and her sister, my aunt Mira. She asked that they take him out on the town to show him around.

He looked scary and was built like a wrestler, but over the next few weeks, my mother and Aunt Mira did show him around. Once, while out, Fred asked Aunt Mira what she would do if someone hurt her sister. She was thrown off, but dismissed the comment and replied, "She's a good person and I don't know why anyone would want to hurt her."

Their evening continued. After being in town for a few weeks, Fred was familiar to everyone. He would stop by and say hello or have dinner with my family and then head home.

When he knocked that morning, he mentioned that his grandmother was asleep and her door was locked. He asked if he could sit at our house until she woke up. Mommy was a little skeptical so she asked him to hold on and went into my aunt's room to wake her and ask her opinion. My aunt replied, "Do what you feel is best."

Mommy decided to let him in. He sat in the living room. Mommy made him comfortable while she continued ironing our clothes. Moments later, she turned around and he was in the doorway of her bedroom, stripped down to his boxers. He had a Rambo-style knife in his hand and came charging at her. He thrust her into a wall, trying to rape her. Mommy put up a fight, but he was a body builder, making the struggles of a 5-foot-5, 120-pound woman pretty useless.

As she was attacked, Mommy banged on the wall to get my aunt's attention. The man was not aware that anyone else was awake. As Mommy continued to bang on the wall while trying to fight him off her, he began stabbing her in the hand.

Mommy got the attention of my aunt, who came into the room asking, "What the hell is going on?" The man was startled, but quickly attacked my aunt, picking her up by the neck and tossing her into a wall. While he was distracted, Mommy ran toward the back of the house to try to get help. Now in the kitchen, she struggled to get the chain lock off the door. He came up behind her and began stabbing her repeatedly all over.

It was as she fought and screamed from the jabs that my 7-year-old brother, Xavier, heard the struggle and screams and woke me to let me know. After I was stabbed, I blacked out for a number of moments. Though the man and the door separated Mommy from me and freedom, she somehow managed to find the strength to get the jammed chain off the door, grab me under her arm and run out of the house.

At that moment, God stepped in and took over. Something that seemed so impossible was made possible. All the neighbors were out in the road, and there to help. My brother had managed to get my Uncle Joe's attention. He went into the house to see if the animal was still around. No luck. He was gone. My aunt and the other kids who had been in the house at the time were safe.

My mother was stretched out on the porch gasping for air. Blood was coming out of her mouth every time she coughed. There was blood all over her clothes, staining the porch. My great-grandmother Ann was there. She said that she had called for an ambulance, but it seemed like hours went by. The emergency medical response team still hadn't showed. Time was running out.

The neighbors grew impatient and started calling for help from their cordless phones, with 911 operators stating that they had never gotten a call. The neighbors insisted and refused to hang up with them until the paramedics arrived. I was sitting on a chair on the porch watching my mom. I had blood all over my nightgown from my mother holding me. When the ambulance finally arrived, they immediately took Mommy away on the stretcher. They then came to check me for wounds, and I was carried into the ambulance as well.

On the ride to the hospital, the medical workers ripped my mother's clothes off and chunks of her flesh fell to the floor of the ambulance, leaving deep holes in her body and her bone exposed.

It reminded me of when I carved holes out of my pumpkin. I was nervous and scared. The medical technicians then came to me and cut my gown off to examine my wounds.

With her bloody hand, my mother reached for my hand and said, "I love you. I want you to watch after your brother." I said, "OK, Momma, I love you too." Bloodstained hands. Sealed with love forever.

I wish that it had been a dream from which I could wake up, or a scary movie on TV from which I could turn to another channel.

If only I had known that this would be our very last conversation, the last time I would hear her voice or touch her. There were many things I did not get to ask or say like, "I am sorry I was not able to help you this time. Who will care for us for the rest of our lives? Who will be there to tuck us in at night? Why wasn't Daddy around to protect us? Who will I be able to consult when I begin to go through puberty or to share my first crush story? Who will I be able to trust to guide me through this thing called life?"

Mommy would miss the major things in my life such as my graduations, first job experiences, my learning how to drive, buying a car, giving birth to her granddaughter, having mommy/daughter days out and traveling together. All of the many times that she felt I misbehaved and I got a beating. I now only wish that those moments had never happened, but could have been filled instead with a lifetime worth of hugs and kisses.

That tragic day, we were both rushed into the emergency room and separated, never to see each other in this lifetime again.

***

Doctors surrounded my bedside and all were moving fast. An oxygen mask was put on my face. My aunt stood nearby trying to keep tears from falling as I tried to ask her what was going on. After a few minutes, I was told to just say my ABCs. I started to feel woozy by the time I got to C. I don't remember quite making it to D.

I woke up to two nurses lifting me off the surgical bed to lay me on another bed in the room I would occupy until I was well enough to leave weeks later. I was in a tremendous amount of pain with a big bandage across my stomach. I learned quickly that anything that forced my stomach muscle to contract — coughing, sneezing, hard crying or moving in certain positions —only caused more pain.

I started to cry for my mother. Only she could take this pain away. She could hold and kiss me and tell me everything was going to be all right. My aunts, friends, brother and a few of my teachers were all at my side. Some were crying and others were praying.

Nurses and doctors were present around the clock. One nurse in particular helped to comfort me. Amazingly beautiful with dark skin and green eyes, she was warm and friendly. She'd read me stories and would come running the moment I hit the button to request help.

The monster that stabbed my mom and me still posed a threat. He was still roaming free on the streets. So, police were posted to patrol the hospital's halls and one of my relatives stayed overnight with me every night.

My aunts Mira and Deidre were at the hospital daily. Mira stayed with me the first night. She tried so hard to hide what was going on, but it showed all over her face. I wanted to see Mommy. Aunt Mira's sitting in the hospital with me and unable to find the words to comfort me were not good signs. She would only respond, "As soon as you are well, you can see her," whenever I said, "Auntie Mira, I want Mommy."

My pain medication kept me drowsy. At least I wouldn't be up for very long in discomfort before I would fall fast asleep. Aunt Mira's son Elijah was only 6 months old at the time. So I figured she would not be able to stay with me at the hospital for very long. But I was scared to be alone and always wondered who would be with me. The one person I really wanted was so close, yet so far. My mommy.

A few days following the attack, the monster, Fred Cunningham, was found in the woods. He was hiding out about three minutes away from our house.

The story made the headlines. He was convicted of five counts of murder and one count of attempted murder. Turns out he had raped and killed two people in other states and was a fugitive hiding out with his family when he attacked me and my family.

For years, until I lost track of it, I carried that newspaper clipping around, trying to make a reality of what for some time still seemed like a bad dream.
So many years later, I sometimes still hang on to the hope of it actually being a dream and not living in my truth. The reality.

FATHERLESS CHILD

My father, who was not always around, showed up to see me with his youngest daughter, my half-sister Joseline, in tow after hearing the news. He had been residing in South Carolina between Orangeburg and Charleston.

Despite the fact that every time he had come to visit my mother, younger brother and me in the past, it had always ended in violence, I wanted my father to stay overnight with me in the hospital. Having my daddy there would give me the comfort I needed.

So I asked him to stay, but he said, "No," telling me he "had things to do." I was so hurt. I felt like I had been punched in the stomach and the stab wounds had reopened. I just wanted the comfort of my parents. To feel protected and loved by the major players who had taken part in creating me.

My nurse always seemed to arrive just in time to distract me from the pain. Rather than giving me painkillers, her being near was a comfort, especially at night when I was having a nightmare.

She had arrived to continue to encourage me to start walking again. I had been using a bedpan with assistance from the nurse. I knew that once I was able to walk, I would be able to go to the bathroom on my own and then make it out of my room to see my mother. This gave me motivation. It started with me just standing, until finally, I made it out the door, down the hall a short way, then to the end of the hall. The pain in my stomach was great and the biggest challenge was standing up straight. The pain increased as the skin was stretched.

During my dad's time with me at the hospital, he made the bed and relaxed while I made a conscience effort to take a few more steps, walking with my nurse. When I got back from my walk, I found that my dad and his daughter had left. I drifted off to sleep. I was awakened by the hospital bill collector's coming for the payment for my hospital cable and phone service.

I kept my money in a box in the drawer next to my bed. I opened the box to pay the bill, and it was empty. My father had stolen all my money. It would be nine years before I would see him again.

FACE TO FACE WITH DEATH

About two weeks passed. One day, during my typical liquid lunch of flavored Jell-O, soup broth and juice, the nurses said it was time to remove the bandage from my stomach. I don't know what I expected when they removed the bandage, but I wasn't ready to relive what still seemed like a bad dream to me. But it was time and they assured me they would take care to try not to hurt me further by pulling the bandage too hard against my skin. I lay there with my eyes closed tight until they gave me the OK to look.

Tears fell from my eyes when I saw the artwork the monster had created. A slash in the middle of my stomach from under my breast down to my belly button, another on a slant beneath my heart, both topped with staples and stitches that would heal overtime. There was also a tube sticking out of the lower left side of my stomach with blood flowing through it. I was horrified. The nurses had to pluck the staples out. I later learned I had had a partial hepatectomy. A portion of my liver had had to be removed due to the stabbing.

God is awesome. With Fred Cunningham's strength and mental state, it could have been worse. He could have put both my mom and me to rest immediately.

My survival is for a purpose and my continued struggles from this experience will soon be of greater use to another.

After what seemed like months of being in the hospital, I was now on my feet, walking a lot better and I insisted on seeing my mother. That day, my favorite fourth-grade teacher, Mr. Akon, came to visit me as he always did, but this time, the look in his eyes was different. He had always projected a sense of being upbeat and happy. Now sadness and unease were all over him. The doctors and nurses came in to tell me that my mom did not make it. I did not understand.

Although I had not been given any information on her progress, I just thought that because I was progressively getting better, that she was. "Once you are able to walk again, you can walk to her," was all people ever told me. Never did I think I was striving to survive while my mother's days were in question, numbered and she was hanging on by a string. I just wanted my mother to walk in and hug me tight. So tight it would wake me from this long nightmare.

That day, my desire to live disappeared. A huge part of me died, and life as I knew it did not seem to be worth living.

Mommy had just turned 26 years old. She was stabbed 28 times the morning of what was to have been her graduation day from nursing school, and she left two kids (a 7- and 9-year-old) behind. She had lost too much blood; even with all the blood donations, it just was not enough. I had known nothing of death before hers. A huge void was left in my heart; hurt, anger and confusion filled me. I could not understand how my mother could be here today and gone forever in the flesh tomorrow.

How could this happen to us? What did I do to deserve this? Is it because I didn't listen or gave her a hard time? Why is there no an age limit or situational allowances that God takes into consideration when He is calling numbers? My mother had children who depended on her. How will we be raised now? God was not being fair. Life was not fair.

I was released from the hospital. The wake and funeral was planned almost immediately after my release. Everyone had to stay with Great-grandma Ann because my house was still the way it had been following the attack, with blood everywhere, and my aunt Deidre's house had recently burned down. Even being as close as we were to my house gave me the creeps. The night I was released from the hospital, I tossed and turned from thoughts of the monster coming back for me. To this day, I am frequently haunted by nightmares.

At the funeral, Mommy looked to be sleeping peacefully. I was just waiting for her to wake up. As I stood next to her casket, many came up to see her, their faces covered in tears. I wanted to cry, too, but I had been told to be strong. I had never attended a funeral. It gave me a clear sense of reality that we are all on borrowed time.

We will meet again in the afterlife, but there will be no more meetings here on earth.

BORN IN TURMOIL

My mother's mom, Grandma Meena, lived in New York and had come down to South Carolina with my mom's brother, Uncle Marvin, and his family soon after getting word about what had happened to her firstborn child.

Grandma Meena herself was the oldest of Great-grandma Ann's children. She got married right out of high school to Grandpa Johnny Beaken. They had three children together: my mother Chara, Marvin and Mira. Grandma later divorced Grandpa, and had a fourth child, Deidre, by another man, Bill Winery.

When my mother was growing up, Grandma Meena had a drinking problem. There were moments when Grandma Meena was alcohol-free, but there were periods when she would drink all night and come in late. Her habits brought on bad behavior and affected her relationship with her children.

It was very hard for them to sleep at night and manage to go to school. However, my mom joined the Reserve Officers' Training Corps while in high school, while my aunt Mira was at the top of her class and played violin. My uncle Marvin, the only boy, found friends and company outside the house, mainly the white boys in the area toward whom he gravitated and learned a lot from. My aunt Deidre, over time, dropped out of school and began to run the streets.

At the tender age of 14, my mom, Chara, met Andrew. He was 20 and a tough, roughneck, street guy. Mommy fell in love with him and it was to him that she gave her virginity. Mommy got pregnant with me at the age of 15. She chose to keep it a secret, as she was afraid to tell her mom. Grandma Meena didn't find out that my mom was pregnant until her belly was poking out. And it was pure punishment after that.

Despite the arguments and verbal abuse, Mommy was able to make it through her pregnancy and my birth. Grandma Meena seemed to finally fully accept the fact that her new grandbaby had arrived and would be in the house because she started supporting Mommy so that she could finish high school. Pictures and stories my grandmother has shared with me confirm that she had me a great deal of the time.

Isn't it amazing how acceptance can change feelings of disappointment and anger overtime, and you can begin to enjoy things much better than you would've first imagined?

Now, Grandma Meena still was not happy at all with my father for not stepping up to the plate and taking on his responsibility. When he came around to see me, verbal arguments would sometimes turn into physical fights, or he would just not be all that interested in me.

My mom came up pregnant again, giving birth to my brother, Xavier, at the age of 18. They say two women can't live in the same household for too long, especially with the situation as it was. All hell broke loose and it was time for Mommy to leave. As Mommy struggled to finish high school and graduate, my grandmother started to come in late, go out drinking and not prepare or provide meals for the household. It got so bad, when Mommy would buy food; she would hide most of it, but would put some out for her brother and sisters.

Grandma Meena was sweet as pie when she was sober. But when she was drinking, she was known to be crazy, violent and impulsive.

There were many late nights when I would find myself walking the floors because I just could not sleep with so much noise in the house. Grandma would come in stumbling drunk and arguing. Most nights, I would go curl up with Aunt Mira as she hummed a tune to help me fall back to sleep. Other nights when Grandma came home drunk, making a lot of noise, I would go to her.

One night, someone tried to come in the house after her. She locked the door and ran to the kitchen to put something in two pots and to turn the stove on. A man was banging on the door. After a while, the banging stopped. While in the kitchen, Grandma pulled up a chair in front of the window. I asked, "What are you doing, Grandma?" She didn't reply. Instead, she grabbed a chair for me to sit down next to her and put her finger to her lips indicating that I should be quiet. We sat in silence. Minutes later, the man who had been banging on the door was at the window, trying to climb in. When he showed his face, Grandma grabbed the pot in which she had been boiling something on the stove and doused him with its contents. The man's screams rang loud as he fell out the window. Grandma then closed the window and took me back to bed.

Another time, we were at her mother's, Great-grandma Ann's, house, and she got into an argument with her boyfriend Mickey. Mickey was also my godfather. The visit was suddenly over. My grandma stabbed him, grabbed me and stormed out to the car. He was coming fast behind us. She put me in the car and strapped me in my seat belt. As she started the car, Mickey tried to stop her. She drove right into him. She got out to check the damage, then hit him again.

Things took a turn for the worst. One morning, my mom was making grits, eggs and bacon for me, Xavier, my aunts Mira and Deidre and my uncle Marvin. Grandma came in with sand all over her and accompanied by her new male friend. Without washing, she came straight to the stove to make her and her friend something to eat. My mother stopped my grandmother in her tracks and told her that she had to wait until our food was prepared before she could have what was left. I must have been around 5 or 6 years old.

Because of my grandmother's previous behavior, I could predict what would happen next. And in any black household with more than one woman, there ALWAYS seems to be issues. My grandmother flipped out, telling my mother that it was her house and her kitchen, and that if she didn't like it, she could get the hell out. Next thing I knew, fists were flying and pots were being thrown. My grandmother attempted to grab the hot pot of grits and throw it on my mother. She was so predictable. She lost this battle when my mother gave her the beatdown she had been giving others for years. My grandma's eye was red —which meant a black eye was coming. She told us to get out.

God says, “Honor thy father and thy mother.” What if the mother in this situation is not playing her role due to a disease that controls her thinking such as alcoholism? Alcohol abuse runs deep in my bloodline.

When my grandmother’s drinking, she often blacks out and has no recollection of what takes place. I know this today, but my mother and her siblings knew it then. So Grandma’s threat was just a threat, but they knew things would not get any better if they continued to stay there.

Mommy managed to find an apartment for us. Grandma moved to New York.

Before she had children, Grandma had visited New York, paving the way for her sisters, Marie, Margaret and Donna, who followed to make better lives for themselves.

After her marriage, Grandma returned South, but would come to New York occasionally to work and visit family. She was no stranger to the city when she decided to move to New York after the fallout with my mom. My uncle Marvin joined her after she got settled.

It would not be until years later, following the unforeseen tragedy, that we would reunite.

INNOCENCE STRIPPED

After Grandma Meena and Uncle Marvin moved to New York City, my aunt Deidre found out she was pregnant at age 15 and gave birth to a baby girl, Nikkia. Though my mother assured her that she would help support her in any way that she could, Deidre decided to move out to live with her daughter's father.

So that just left Mommy and Aunt Mira. Aunt Mira and Mommy were not only sisters, but also best friends.

Aunt Mira, who played violin and often serenaded me as a child on nights when I couldn't sleep and had instead found my way into her bed, was my favorite. After graduating high school, she enrolled in Job Corps. During one of her visits home from the Corps, she met a man named Bob who lived across the street from us. Bob was kind. He was a Rastafarian and had the longest dreadlocks. He drove a white car and lived in big, two-story house. My aunt seemed so happy with him. He helped pay for her to attend Job Corps in Jacksonville, Fla., and when she came home to visit, we would often meet at his place for Sunday dinners. Soon enough, Aunt Mira found out she was pregnant with their son, Elijah. After graduating from Job Corps, she returned to Orangeburg and moved in with Bob.

Now it was just my mom, my brother and I. We moved a lot, but my mother would make every apartment nice and cozy.

As a child, many things didn't register or make sense. As an adult and having a better understanding, I know now that there were many things I shouldn't have been exposed to. I was the kid who was always in the midst of things.

My father would come by every once in a while to see us. He was a drug dealer and a user. Not sure how that worked out. But my dad would come over and I just wanted to be around him. I would walk into the room and he would have his mouth filled with smoke and his expanded jaws made him look like a blowfish. Next to him on the table, would be tubes and pipes and the smell in the room was one that I have never forgotten. It was a strong alcohol scent. He would quickly shoo me away. Then exhale and immediately fire up the tube and inhale filling his jaws to look like a blowfish again. Not realizing I was still there, he would look at me until he fell into a daydream.

My mom seemed to never show any feelings on things that were going on in her life. She was such a strong woman. She did the very best she could under the circumstances and embraced all other situations as well that came her way. She was a mother and a big sister to her siblings and also helped to care for the niece and nephew that the family was blessed within such a short time. There are blessings in every bit of hardship you feel.

My mother rarely went out. I remember the one time she did go out with her school friends. My aunt watched us and the end result of her night out was horrible. My sleep was interrupted by the cries of my mother and a man in the living room. My mom had been kidnapped and was almost gang raped. She tried to defend herself but still received a blow to the mouth and lost her front tooth. But it turned out that the man who was supposed to be the first to have his way with her was someone that was familiar to her. He had no clue as to what he was walking in to. He saw my mother and immediately came to her rescue and called it off. He brought her home, emotionally traumatized, but safely. Although she endured some type of pain, God presented himself in a way no man could have and covered her. HE protected her from further injuries, possible diseases and/or death.

Perhaps that is why Mommy always kept a watchful eye on us. She was very protective and strict. We were only allowed to go outside in front of the house to play with friends.

We were living in a two-family house on Glover Street, and a good friend of mine was a little girl named Ashley who lived next door. We would go out and stand on the sidewalk and try to get the attention of the eighteen-wheeler truck drivers so they would honk their horns. That was our everyday plan and was the most exciting part of our playing together.

One day, we were outside playing with her ball when it flew into the street. Without looking to make sure there were no cars coming, she ran after it and got hit by a car.

It hurt to know that my friend was hurt. I saw her get put in an ambulance, but no one ever told me any details about what happened to her. I asked but I would be quickly shushed and told not to bring it up. I remember her shoe being left in the street. When I see shoes or clothes in the street now as an adult, it often makes me think of her and if someone got hit and their belongings were left behind. As time went on, no one ever mentioned Ashley and I never saw her again. It was as if the situation never happened and she never existed.

Crazy how life goes on, but the residue of an experience lives inside of you. Especially if it's not addressed.

Moving around from house to house as we did, we needed to take the school bus to get to school at Revlon Elementary. Sometimes the bus would arrive later than scheduled, throwing Mommy's schedule off, so she would ask her younger sister, my aunt Deidre, to wait with me and put me on the bus some days.

But some days, instead of putting me on the bus, Aunt Deidre would lie and tell my mom I was sick or that we had missed the bus just so she could play in my private areas. She would make it into a game and play with my clitoris and put her finger in my vagina. It was uncomfortable, but I didn't quite know it was wrong because it was my aunt. I finally told my mom and she never left me with Aunt Deidre again.

Sometimes protection is needed from the ones right under one's nose. And the abuse would come back to haunt me.

There was a family we used to play with across the street; my mom also spent time with their parents. The kids would often come over to play with my brother and me. That all came to an end when one day, we were in the basement and one of the boys, Neo, started fondling me. Mothers always know when something is wrong. We were too quiet. When my mother came downstairs I was on top of him, dry humping him, similar to things I had witnessed. The treatment by my aunt primed my response when Neo touched me. When kids do things, you have to wonder where they get it.

My mother came downstairs and Neo and I both jumped up, our faces gone blank. Caught! She asked no questions. She sent me to my room to wait by my bed butt naked until she came for me. This meant she would be there to beat me very shortly. The torture was in the waiting because it would at times take me falling sleep or having dinner and a bath before she spanked me.

She called Neo's family and told them what she had seen and that he was no longer allowed to play with me and my brother again. My mother was delirious. I would have been dead if she had attacked me right then with the anger and rage she felt. Instead time went by and she told me to take a bath, eat some dinner and then go to bed. This gave her time to calm down. I was on my way to bed when she leaped on me and tore my behind up. The strap was put to my natural behind. She threatened to tell my father. I was scared as all hell and really didn't know why because he had never laid a finger on me.

My father ironically had popped up to visit. I thought my telling my dad what had happened before she could tell him what I had done, would make my punishment lighter. Her beating me was harsh enough. But when he found out that Mommy had already beaten me, he beat her up for hitting me. I was so scared and didn't quite understand what was going on or that this would have been his response. He always found a reason when he came over to start an argument to fight her. This time he beat her real bad. He would beat her like she was his equal.

My dad came from a decent family. He was one of five boys and one girl, my aunt Gail. Both Grandma Meena and his mom, Grandma Flore, were good friends. While Grandma Meena didn't think highly of my dad, she had a lot of respect for his family. Grandma Flore was very much interested in being actively involved in our lives regardless of whether her son was. We looked forward to our Christmas vacation being spent with her in Charleston. That was one of the only times Mommy allowed my brother and me to stay out of the house. This gave her a small break as well. Grandma Flore always told me that having all of us around for the holidays made the holidays more special and joyful.

Sometimes my parents' relationship was anything but joyful. One night, my dad had come by and watched us while Mommy stepped out. As time passed, he grew angrier. He went in the hallway and put window screens on the step and a knife under the sofa. He was hoping that Mommy would come up the steps, not notice the screens and slip and fall back down the steps. She was smarter than that. When she came in, they argued and he went for the knife under the sofa, which my brother and I had already managed to grab and give to Mommy for her to protect herself. That day she not only stabbed him but fought him like he was her equal.

We already knew the routine of him only coming around periodically after he left. There were times we would need food or money and would pay a visit to where he hung out. Mommy would take us with her when she had to run him down for money to take care of us, thinking he would feel guilty and give us what we needed. One day he was with a woman said to be his girlfriend who was apparently jealous of our very being. That day she and my mother had words and then a fight broke out. My mother beat her so bad; she left a hole in her cheek from biting her. The cops took Mommy to jail, along with my brother and me. We had to wait there with her for someone to come get us or for Mommy to post bail. My father never took sides. He wasn't manly enough or fit to even take us until Mommy got out of what he had been the cause of. He just sat back and watched the catfights. He never stood up to defend us.

As we got older, my mother would allow us to go further than the front yard to play with friends. I would hang out with a couple of friends I went to school with on their porch, playing cards often. I remember getting into a fight with these twin girls. They had jumped me and I came home crying. My mother had always said,

"You better fight back. Bigger or smaller, it did not matter. You better had tried your hardest. If it is more than one, you better get one of them down and do serious damage. Fight dirty. That is why there are bricks, sticks, and bottles lying around." If I did not fight and came home crying like a baby then I would have to come home and fight with her. So, I came home crying and told her I tried my best. She didn't believe me and dragged me back outside to find these girls. They were scared to fight again but my mother insisted. So when I got to them it was on and popping. It was an all-out battle. I never had a problem with those girls again.

I've had few fights in my lifetime. I tend to blackout during the blows and never recall what happens. As I am sure is normal. The thoughts I have when thinking of protecting myself would land me in jail. A quick technique to impair my enemy. I often think of strangling or squeezing the life out of someone who attacks me. Snapping a neck or breaking a few bones. It often plays in my head and keeps me on defense. Losing control of my mind or myself is something I fear. So, I try to stay clear of drama and confrontation.

We moved to a brick house on Stroman Street that was attached to this evil lady. She was a miserable old fart who didn't have any family that visited her. She would roll her eyes when she saw us. Not quite the welcoming neighbor.

We didn't have much but the pieces of furniture we did have were priceless to us. I often wanted company other than my brother, who would always want to fight. Most days I played outside by myself. My brother would be out playing with friends. I was often bored with very little to keep me occupied. Mommy would want us to take daily naps when I wasn't tired. So, I found myself getting into mischief. She would tell me not to do something without any explanation as to why not, and I would do it anyway. One day, I burned the back of her sofa. It was so soft and furry. My excuse for doing it was that I wanted to see how fast it would flame up. Another time, she told me not to touch the unstable wall unit shelf that held a 13-inch television with a wire hanger in the back to get a clear picture. There was no remote that came with the television because it was an old-school black and white. One where you had to turn the knob. I touched it anyway and the television came crashing down. I just didn't learn. I got my redbone tail torn up for both.

One thing about this house, it made Santa more believable to my brother and I. We had a chimney and fireplace. Every year when Christmastime came around, my mother would get extra creative. We just had a tree and decorations. The gifts she was able to get for us would be stored in the backyard, in the shed or at my aunt's house. This particular Christmas, she put us to bed early, and wrapped and placed all of our gifts under the tree she had on the back porch. We woke up the next morning and there was a hole in the glass by the door and the cookies and milk were gone. We questioned it. Mommy said it was the reindeers getting impatient outside while Santa was inside talking to her eating cookies. For some time, I believed that, until my dad opened his mouth about Mommy not letting him in to see us so he had kicked the glass in. Mommy tried her best to protect us from all harm from outsiders. However, the most harm was from my father. Her chosen poison.

The evil old lady next door and Mommy had gotten into it one day and shortly after, our house caught on fire. I have no recollection of how the house fire started. We came home to it. Now we had to move again.

We moved into a trailer on Edisto Drive near my great-grandmother Ann. It was spooky because it was at the end of the road by the woods. Throughout the time there, I had helped care for two pigs. I looked forward afterschool to feeding them their slop and watching them play in the mud. We lived a couple houses away from Ms. Cunningham. She was my great-grandma Ann's best friend. She had a lot of chicken in her yard just as my grandma had. It was said that she would cast spells on some folk when they walked past her house. We were so afraid we would run past her house.

I had gotten familiar with my new environment quick. Met new friends in the area to play with. After school, I would play hopscotch, jump rope, go bike riding and just enjoy time spent with my friends and some of my cousins who lived directly across from Great-grandma Ann.

Summer was the best time at Great-grandma Ann's. My cousins from New York would come down and I would have even more company to play with every day. My mother would mind all the girls, while the boys would stay with Great-grandma Ann.

Every Sunday was church. Morning and evening service. My great-grandma was dating the deacon, and it was pure punishment to be there day in and day out. We would fall asleep in church or talk and get the evil stares from Great-grandma and the ushers. After church we all took turns washing off in the tin on the back porch. We would change into play clothes and have watermelon in the yard. Something we all looked forward to.

Great-grandma had a chicken coup in the back of her house. I am not a big fan of chicken. I am not sure if it is because I had too much of it growing up or if it was the experience before getting it in the pot for dinner that turned me off. Each day that chicken would be on the menu, we would pick a number of who would go in. Once we caught the chicken, we would have to hold its legs, feet and neck while Great-grandma cut the neck off. Blood would be everywhere, even on me. She would then skin and cook it.

There were also days when frog legs and rabbit meat was on the menu. I couldn't help but to think that there was no discrimination or mercy on the animals chosen to keep a meal on the table. I remember a snake being on her ceiling and she snatched him up and killed it. As if this is normal, she would sit and tell me the best angle to grab and kill them. I'm not sure if it made it in the pot but I made it a point to not stay for dinner that day.

Although it was the only environment I had known, I hated the many bugs that would feed on me. There were the mosquitoes, red ants, gnats, flies and the furry caterpillars. The mosquitoes would suck on me leaving me scratching for days. All I ever heard was "Don't scratch it because it will leave cat ball marks." I was not concerned what scars would be left because all I understood was getting that itch to stop. The red fire ants would bite my feet and it would sting and itch. I had to sit in the tin on the porch to stop the burning and itching. Being a city girl now, I can do without animals and bugs of any sort. I don't like any discomfort that they may cause for even a second.

There were so many fun moments we had with our cousins when they came down. One day my mom took us all to the park and we started a baseball game. Marquees, Chastity and Carrie were cheating and a fight broke out. My brother jumped in and it was war. He was always a beast and it didn't help that he was overprotective. It was the North against the South. We quickly hashed it out and were playing all over again. That is the beauty of being kids. There was not much to do looking back on it now, but we made the very best of everything. Just having other kids to look forward to playing with as a child, was exciting. It was very boring otherwise. Once they had left to come back to New York, life went back to normal and I rarely stayed at my great-grandmother's unless my mom needed to go somewhere.

And even that came to a screeching end when one day, Great-grandma Ann was watching me and decided to go down the road to visit a friend named Mrs. Emily's. One of Mrs. Emily's nephews was also visiting. When introducing me, my great-grandmother told me to go over and give him a hug. I was nervous and refused, but she forced me. I very shyly walked over and he not only hugged me, but picked me up and put me on his lap.

As they continued talking to each other, he pulled me in between his legs and started gyrating his hips. His penis was so hard it was hurting my butt. I managed to scream and pushed my way off of him. I ran so fast out of that house until I made it home, which was at the other end of the road. I waited there until my mother came home. It seemed like forever before she did. I told my mom what happened and when she approached my great-grandma, she accused me of lying. This was something that often took place in the past in the South, to cover up wrongdoing. It protects the predator and destroys the prey. Without any further discussion, we didn't associate with my great-grandmother much anymore.

****

Soon after my aunt Mira had her son Elijah, my mother learned that his father, Bob, had been arrested and that Aunt Mira needed a place to live.

There was a vacant house that had become available right behind my Great-grandma Ann's house. It was really nice. It had three bedrooms with a front and back yard. It also had a fireplace. So we were all back together again. Aunt Mira and her new baby boy Elijah had their own room, my brother and me shared a room and my mom had her own room. It was a very cozy new beginning. The best part was that the pigpen was not too far for me to go see them, and feed and play with them.

In the summer months, my brother and I were responsible for raking the leaves in the yard and winter months our primary job was to cut wood for the fireplace. One day, I had finished cutting my wood and my brother hadn't even started cutting his share. I went in to let Mommy know that I had finished mine. Xavier was right behind me. She asked him if he had finished his and he didn't answer. After trying and failing to get him to respond for a few minutes, she furiously went for her belt. When she returned, she tried to get him to respond again. Again he did not respond. In fact, he just stared at her. She swung the belt to hit him and to her surprise he balled up his fist and hit her back. I was told to go to my room and she tore his behind up.

This behavior was new coming from my brother. He was now emulating what he saw my father do to my mother. By this time, there weren't many visits from my father. I later found out that he was in and out of jail, had gotten hit by a car and was in a coma. God works in mysterious ways because before this happened, me, my brother and mom were in the park kiting and Daddy came by to pick Xavier up for a while. When Daddy brought him back, he had white powder under his nose. I asked what it was, but from my mother's expression I knew that it wasn't good. We were told to go fly the kites together while she talked to him about the white powder. I knew it didn't end well because he didn't kiss or tell us goodbye.

A few months before the tragedy, Grandma Meena and my mom finally spoke after not doing so for a few years. Mommy learned that Grandma had gotten clean after going to her AA meetings and was working at Harlem Hospital. She had apologized for all that had happened and then asked her if the money she had been sending every month to her mom, Great-grandma Ann, to give to us was helping with all the household expenses. She had been sending it to her mom because we moved around frequently. Her mom's address was stable and she had spoken with her mother daily.

My mother had no knowledge of the funds because the money had never been received or mentioned. They were both furious and confronted Great-grandma Ann. All they got from her was that there was a fee to send mail through her address. She had become conniving. This explained her actions the day of the tragedy when we needed help and she claimed she called 911. Instead she asked us what did we want her to do for us as my mother gasped for air with blood coming out of her mouth.

My mother had struggled to take care of herself, her children and siblings. The hardship she experienced could have possibly been lessened if the monies had been received. Money is the root to all evil. My grandma Meena had planned to come to South Carolina to clear the air and make amends with her children that summer. However, that was not in God's plan. It almost seemed as if it was a punishment for my grandma Meena.

How can one live with the hurt and pain of knowing how wrong they had done someone that is their own flesh and blood? Let alone their children. Now that she no longer exists here on earth, an enormous of amount of guilt began to set in.

After the funeral and my graduation from my fourth grade year, we were on the highway headed north to New York City. Saying good-bye to the pigs was the hardest thing next to losing my mom. I just wanted to sit with them and cry the tears I felt I had to keep in because I was told to be strong.

It seemed that life was a much better place to live in New York. Everyone that came to visit the South always looked like they were from the videos I would see when I was at a friend's house. I later realized that most of the videos of rappers and singers where taped in New York. The New York slang and fashion was very different compared to my then Southern lazy accent and at times running around shoeless.

New York is where dreams were made a reality. Where my new life began.

Lord I Ask Why….

What did I do to deserve this?
To have witness such a horrific tragedy
That ultimately took her away to be missed

With frequent haunting nightmares of that day
And eye for eye or a deeper understanding as to why
I often wish there was a higher penalty for him to pay
But realized the judicial system doesn't work that way

I have been unsuccessful getting answers, so I turn to you
I am your child that you allowed to suffer physically, mentally and emotionally
Leaving lifelong scars that holds as a daily reminders of endless pain

Do YOU exist?
Trying to find the reasoning as to why she had to go
Then my father stealing from me
I'm sure hoping to never be seen anymore
Abandonment and rejection lives in my heart with pain
So I ask, "How does one know that YOU exist?"

The many sayings that people have made reference to:

- What doesn't kill you make you stronger
- HE doesn't give one more than they can handle
- HE wouldn't bring me this far to leave me

In the midst of it all, none of these sayings is clearly understood or used as inspiration to keep pushing forward. It becomes clear and well received overtime after reflecting on how it relates to you in your many walks of life.

Life is said to be a gift. A gift that keeps on giving, if you're truly living. Suffering with many obstacles, heartache and pain from loss through death or relationships but the strongest survives. It is hard to consider it a gift when much of our lives consist of struggle. Life is filled with challenges and decisions but there is no greater victory than when you have taken chances, learned from your mistakes and standing at the top of that mountain with sweat, blood and tears of joy from achieving destiny.

ADJUSTMENTS —NEW CITY, NEW LIFE

Life took a drastic turn. June 1989. I arrived in New York with my brother Xavier, Grandma Meena, Aunt Mira with her baby boy, Elijah, Uncle Marvin and his baby boy, Peter, and girlfriend, Odel.

Given the slow pace and limited diversity of the small town of Orangeburg, South Carolina, you can imagine the culture shock and huge adjustments ahead. I only knew of country living, and city life was different to the extreme. I had known houses surrounded by grass and reached by dirt roads within quiet communities with relatively few people. I had had the run of a mini farm complete with pigs, horses, cows and the inhabitants of my great-grandmother's chicken coop. In my new city home, sky-high apartment buildings surrounded by concrete were everywhere. There were few homes like the kind I was used to back in South Carolina. And the phrase "the city never sleeps" lived up to its name.

Grandma Meena had gained full custody of my younger brother, and me and we had relocated to Harlem, where most of my family lived. On top of not having my mom, I was now forced to live where it was overpopulated and the buildings looked condemned.

My grandma did not have a place of her own to stay, so we bunked with her sister Donna and Donna's boyfriend. Aunt Mira met a guy who became her boyfriend, and she soon moved in with him.

Aunt Donna was my grandmother's younger sister. She too had issues with alcoholism. Like many, she was the sweetest when she was sober. However, when she was drunk, she exhibited a dangerous kind of mischievousness. One day, I was sitting in the living room talking to my brother, when an intoxicated Aunt Donna playing with a set of nunchakus, threw them, and hit me in the back of my head.

People never seem to be at fault when they are fully incapable of their actions. Bad acts are always blamed on their current condition.

The number of incidents that occur while under the influence is limitless and should not be taken lightly.

My grandma Meena was the best. She did her best to make life comfortable for us. The situation was hard for her as well, coping with the pain of our loss and giving up her life to raise her grandchildren. It was difficult and her efforts were much appreciated.

Now, Grandma did have a man in her life as well. Glen was his name. He was about her age. He used to hang out on the corner of West 137th Street and Lenox Avenue. He had the softest voice and seemed so gentle with my grandma. Very different from most of the men I had seen in her life. But my grandma's makeup had changed from when she lived in the South when I was younger. She was back in church and clean.

Returning to the North with my brother and me, things were difficult. Due to the amount of time she had spent in South Carolina taking care of us, she had had to give up the job she had at the hospital. My mom had never worked a job long enough for us to collect Social Security after her death, and neither did my dad.

So we had to depend on the city's social services to survive. It was such a miserable process, so many appointments and a lot of running around, dealing with the system.

****

My tragedy is my testimony and my scar on my stomach is my tattoo of remembrance of my mommy and survival. I had to relive it more often than not. There was no getting around it. At times, I felt I was always made an exhibit. My grandma would make me stand up and show the artwork on my stomach to company, or when at the doctor's office, go in to great details about a day I wish never happened. I rarely looked at my stomach. With the way that it healed, it was like a dark worm stapled and stitched, beginning in the center of my chest and crawling down to my belly button. Another appeared on my side under my heart, born of the scar from the tube that had transported blood in and out of my body. So I had no desire to look at it or show it, as I got older. If only there was something more that I could have done that day. The reality of it all is, if I had tried anything, the situation could have ended differently and I may not be here to tell this story.

****

Our stay at Aunt Donna's house was short. At the end of that first summer, Grandma Meena checked us in to a shelter in Lower Manhattan on Catherine Street. It was the longest and most horrific experience, but one that became increasingly familiar.

There were about 20 cots lined up next to each other in a large room filled with the needy. My grandma would sit up while we slept to keep us safe. There were many nights I couldn't sleep. So I would be up witnessing many things a child shouldn't see.

I saw a man tie a rubber band around his arm and stick a needle in. The noise he made before he got his fix awoke others, causing a scene. Another night, a different drug user keeled over after getting his fix, shaking with a bunch of white froth coming out of his mouth. Shelter staff pulled him and other users like him out, trying hard not to disturb everyone else.

It was extremely scary. There was an open-door policy, with all in need served on a first come, first serve basis. It did not matter your situation. But space was limited. When I saw the movie "Pursuit of Happyness" with Will Smith and his son Jaden, I quickly remembered our situation being similar. Falling on hard times doesn't discriminate. Life happens and how you respond and bounce back means much more than always being on top and in a good place. This shows resilience and brings out other sides you may not have known existed. I know some who were always on top and when life happened, they jumped off the roof, committing suicide or became one of the "too proud homeless" that will not go for the help that is provided but rather pity themselves and want others to have pity on them as well. Experiences are designed to build character and strength within oneself.

Conditions at our shelter were not only unfit and unsanitary for families, they were unjust. Once we would leave in the mornings, we would have to make it back on time and comply with all of the rules to get put on a list to be placed in a hotel until housing was found for us. The hotels would change, but our favorite was our stay at the Saratoga in Queens. Our stay there was pretty long. As time went by and we were making it back inside before curfew, we became eligible for overnight passes. And Grandma Meena made it a point to take us to visit Aunt Mira and Elijah, as well as Grandma Meena's sisters and our cousins. She also made a very nice Christmas for us during our stay at the Saratoga.

Every hotel change meant enrolling in a new school, because how much time we would spend at a hotel and the distance of the hotel to our school was not dictated by the school we were already attending.

It was difficult communicating and making friends. I couldn't relate to the other children. I was extremely angry. Kids talk about their family, animals, and toys, other possessions. My mom was gone; my dad had walked out, was hardly ever around and had another child he was caring for. It seemed that the only adjustment to be made for me was moving to the big city. Being unstable was familiar. In South Carolina, I had moved around from house to house. Now, in the city, I didn't know how long I would be staying in any one hotel or any school.

Finally, after what seemed like an eternity of being moved around from place to place and school to school for nine months, in April 1990, we were placed in permanent housing in the Bronx. The majority of my relatives were living in Harlem. We were the first to move across the bridge. The Bronxdale housing projects were different from many of the other places I had called home. Our apartment was in a building surrounded by a cluster of other buildings. It was a two-bedroom apartment. My brother had his own bedroom, while I shared a bedroom with my grandmother. I was very happy with this, considering my frequent nightmares.

Now that we were in our permanent housing, Grandmother took us around the area scouting for schools. Community School 152 was on Evergreen and Bruckner. We were tested. Due to our scores, my brother and I were forced to attend different schools. The unfairness of the system. We were brother and sister, why was it not possible to attend the same school? Make it easier for a parent to better manage and maintain visits and schedules. My brother was placed in a different school district entirely. Public School 47 was the school that most of our friends in the projects attended. But our two schools were located in different directions, which made it difficult for my family to get us to school on time. My grandmother was determined to make it work. My uncle Marvin would walk me to school, and Grandma would take Xavier on her way to work. She had started working as a home health aide. She was determined to provide us with stability so that we could all begin to heal.

With my uncle taking me to school, I was able to make some changes to my school attire. I would have him stash my Converses in his backpack for me. I hated some of the footwear my grandmother would make me wear. I was a tomboy and she would always have shoes out for me to wear. He never told our secret.

Uncle Marvin had just gone through a very trying time in his life with his family. His family split causing him to further lose his mind. The apartment they shared when I had first arrived in New York City was in Harlem near my aunts. It was a beautiful apartment in a brownstone building. At the time he was working in Harlem Hospital. When we lived in the shelter, we had made it a point to visit him every weekend when we got our weekend passes. His son, Peter, was the cutest little boy, bow legged and pigeon toed. He was born on my mother's birthday, and he and Elijah, Aunt Mira's baby boy, were just months apart in age.

Our tragedy remained fresh and everyone was dealing with it in his or her own way, but it seemed to help to have everyone together to spend time and break bread.

When things worsened in Uncle Marvin's family, he moved in with us. Over the course of time, not being able to see his son, Peter, affected him tremendously.

And during this time, Grandma seemed to have been holding up well but she started to lose weight and it was becoming obvious that she was beginning to have trouble.

We started off well in school. This was now the fourth school in the fifth grade that I had attended. I was a loner and was perfectly fine with that, considering all that I had just experienced. Kids would come to my table during lunch and invite me into their circle, but I had no interest.

The overall nature and attitudes of most New Yorkers I met were not at the level of friendliness I was used to in South Carolina.

There were so many different ethnic and racial groups. I am African American, but have been mistaken for Hispanic, or mixed with Asian or Caucasian. Being light-skinned with green eyes and nappy, sandy brown hair did not exactly scream "black girl." But I grew to be a bit prejudiced against Hispanics. I was at a lunch table next to a group of them one day, when almost immediately, they switched from English to Spanish. I kindly asked, "Why did you immediately change your language when I came around? That's rude." One responded in a not-so-friendly tone, "Maybe we are talking about you." I immediately got defensive and was determined at some point to learn the language.

As I have matured, I have realized you can't let one bad apple spoil it for all. I have met some of the friendliest, down-for-you and have-your-back Hispanics whom I am cool with today. Most of my neighbors are Hispanic. This was a test from God to make me a better person. To accept everyone without prejudice.

But as a child in my new school, finding acceptance was a challenge. One group of boys was just so mean. Curly, Larry and Moe were their nicknames. They would get a good laugh about anything. They didn't discriminate, so anyone could be a target.

From your attire, hairstyle, physical impairments, you name it; they made a joke about it. I couldn't stand the very sight of them or going to school because of them. Today, I realize that the people who get picked on the most are usually liked by the bully or turn out to become greater beings in life.

My class included an interesting group of people. There was this one girl who befriended me. She was what we black folks call "high yellow" in complexion and talkative with a huge gap between her teeth. Her name was Zamia. She was really nice, though no one seemed to care for her. She was different and very comfortable in her skin. She often came to school looking like a bag of Skittles. Just colorful, with stripes and poker dots. But because she did all the talking, our friendship happened quickly. I admired her confidence and free spirit. Something about which I knew nothing.

Then there was Rosa. She was Hispanic. We would come to school and the first stop every day would be to the bathroom to make up her face and comb her hair down. Her pants were so tight; they looked like they were painted on. I was like the flunky who would just sit and wait while she get dolled up for the day though I had no desire to mimic her. She had the boys going crazy. Looking back on it, she looked too old to be in our grade.

I met my first friend Ayana. She was really nice. Now, she was one person I could fully talk to. For a fifth grader, she had the prettiest penmanship. It looked like a teacher's handwriting. We connected very well. I mean this was my first real friend. She understood me. She would come to my house to play with me and I would go to hers. My uncle Marvin would take us to the park just so we could spend time together outside of school.

Things were going well for the month that we knew each other until one day I called her house because she was supposed to come visit me, and her number had been disconnected. She didn't show up to class anymore. I had my Uncle Marvin take me to her house to see if she and her family still lived there and was told that they had moved. I was so hurt, frustrated and angry all at once. The pain of losing someone had resurfaced. That was the end of what I thought would be a lifetime friendship. She had left before the school year ended. I was slowly learning that nothing good lasted forever, but the hurt brought about by such change seemed to be both intense and extensive.

But I have grown to learn that just because something or someone is stripped away from you, it does not mean that it or that person is gone for good. Not sure how, but many years later, Ayana and I reunited. She had relocated to Staten Island. We picked up where we left off and filled each other in on our lives. She had just met the love of her life and was planning her wedding. I was taken aback when she asked me to be a bridesmaid in her wedding. I was pregnant at the time, but made the best-looking pregnant bridesmaid ever. Despite having to deal with morning sickness so bad I had to keep a set of Ziploc bags handy, it was a beautiful wedding and I was so happy to be part of such a personal and amazing event with someone I deemed to be like a sister.

She was studying to be a nurse and was super busy just as I was also, working full time, attending Lehman college full time for my bachelor's degree and expecting a baby. So we did not get to speak as much as we would have liked, but nonetheless, we reached out when we could. At my baby shower, I took the opportunity to ask if she and her husband would be the godparents to my new bundle. They were excited and said yes. Time went by and we lost contact yet again. We recently, through Facebook, reunited eight years later. Again, we picked up where we left off and I was so excited to learn that she had her first beautiful little boy Brian. We are determined not to lose contact again.

When things or people in your life are meant to be, nothing and no one can come between that. When it's good, you can just pick up where you left off and continue building.

One of my signature sayings over the years has been, "Now is not a good time. However, if it is meant to be I will see you again at a better time." I use this in many instances of my life, and it seems to work in most cases, which is interesting. If I want something and my pockets do not agree, it simply means it is not meant for me to have. However, if it is there when I come back and my pockets are right, then I know it is meant for me to have. Timing and patience are everything.

****

Another of my childhood friends was Asia. She became my best friend in the Bronxdale Houses. As a child, every friend became my best friend. She was in a different class from me, but on our way to and from school, we would see each other. Despite my anger, attitude and a feeling of being in my own world of misery, she was someone who cared enough to stick around and get to know me. She asked if I lived in Bronxdale, and once I said yes, she asked if we could walk to school together and (to let her tell it to this present day) supposedly, I was evil and said yes, but gave her the wrong apartment number. She says I sat and watched her go to the wrong door and did not say anything and just laughed at her. That was the start of a friendship like no other. We participated in music chorus together, played in the cafeteria and playground. After school and on the weekends, I would go to her house to hang out. I was starting to feel comfortable about opening up again and somehow it felt natural. I would go to her house to practice for talent shows. Her sister Mia was our choreographer. She was older. I thought she was such a mean person because she used to pick on me all the time, calling me names, hurting my feelings. We spent many nights practicing with her sister Mia for our talent shows. She would scream at me until I got the dance right. Now I realize that was just her personality. Years have gone by and when I would see her in church, we exchange the warmest hugs. Not having had an older sibling, I didn't realize that it is just the way they show their love.

We would have the newest dances to present to our audience. We had the backward running man and this dance that required her, because I was lighter, to throw me over her back to "Turn It Out" by Rob Base. We would practice often until it was perfected. One day in the gym, me and this Hispanic boy named Rick were practicing the dance, when he had to flip me over his back and I fell the wrong way, right on my neck. Ouch! The pain was so excruciating. I was sore for a while, but managed to get it together in time for the show.

I realized at that moment that I really enjoyed performing and having an audience.

Asia and I had a similar physique. She was slim and tall with long limbs just like me. The only difference was that she was dark-skinned. People used to call us Pam and Gina, the characters from the Martin Lawrence comedy sitcom, or Cindy and Sharay from the movie "House Party" because we danced well. We spent a lot of time over the year taking long walks to the supermarket or to Southern Boulevard to shop. We even chilled on the corner by our building, when either one of us was supposed to be going to the store, to just talk about nothing in particular.

As we completed elementary and moved into junior and senior high school, we attended our junior and senior proms with our dates together. As we got older and proved to be responsible, we made our way down to the infamous Numero Uno on 116th Street and Lexington Avenue in East Harlem and took signature "vanilla and chocolate" pictures with similar outfits, khakis with V-neck sweaters. Although similar, we still had our own style. I wore my uptown Nikes and she had on her Timberland moccasins. We would write letters to each starting with a page heading indicating the date, current activity and location, which was hilarious because most of mine took place in the bathroom. Whether I was using it or not that, the bathroom was where I found peace and serenity.

Hanging out at Asia's house also was my escape from all that was starting to go on in my house. Her mother and father were together and she had a brother and a sister. It was the kind of family life I craved.

By this time, my aunt Mira was pregnant with her second child and was having problems with her boyfriend, Steve. So, she had come to stay with us. Things were going well until she and Grandma Meena got into an argument one night. Grandma put her out, and the relationship that had started since we had reunited after the tragedy was back to zero. It was never the same after that. Aunt Mira had made amends with her boyfriend and went back to the house they shared. Soon after, she gave birth to a little boy she named Isaiah.

Uncle Marvin's struggles had grown. He was starting to talk to himself, and at times, he did not recognize me. He was having full-fledged conversations and would laugh out loud to himself. He would often stare at me, talk to himself, and then answer me when I would interrupt. Things worsened and his conversations became filled with anger and foul language. I would say, "Hey Uncle." He would respond, "This b*tch said, Hey." I would ask whom was he talking to and he would answer, "Hey, Champ," or "Hey, Baby Girl. Are you OK? What's wrong?" as if those questions should be addressed to me. I wasn't afraid because I knew and loved him dearly, and knew he meant well and wouldn't do anything to harm me. But as the years passed, his condition got progressively worse. It was embarrassing when my friends would ask me if he was crazy. There was a time when he cut his hair into a Mohawk, zeeked his hairline and had a matted dread lock as a rat-tail; my friends would laugh at him because of the way he looked. It bothered me so when they would laugh, but I didn't know any better and just simply wanted to fit in. So I made light of the situation, made it seem as if it didn't bother me and laughed with them.

I loved my uncle and grandma, but was very ashamed of my in-house situations and their behaviors. As an adult, it is easy to accept that we are who we are. As a child that is not understood.

****

My years at Junior High School 123 were my favorite among my school days. Most of my graduating class attended Junior High School 123 as we were all in the same school district. This made adjusting to the new school from elementary quite easy.

Before my family's final placement in Bronxdale, there had not been many points in my life where I could recall living in one place too long. This affected my level of comfort and ability to truly relax and unpack all my boxes, as it were. My school days were different. I attended the same head start and elementary school until fourth grade. Then, though there were many schools for fifth grade due to our living situation at the time, once we got settled at Bronxdale, it was basically one school straight through to graduation.

Today, I am very big on structure and stability. Longevity is what I strive for.

In my first year of junior high, I had wonderful teachers who took a special interest in me. Different from my previous teachers in earlier grades. Once, my grandmother had come to school and threatened to put my teacher's head threw a chalkboard when I got a bad grade on my report card. My teacher was so scared, she made me teacher's helper and I never had a grade issue or misunderstanding again.

Junior high school was different. My English teacher, Mrs. Harriet, was from the South. She was a calm, patient and caring teacher. She chose the perfect profession. She assisted me with word pronunciation and taught me New York English lingo 101. I not only sounded country, but had a touch of Geechie as well, from my father. I had issues with pronouncing words beginning with "str" or "scr" such as string, strong and script. I would pronounce them as scring, scrong and stript. Shrimp would be pronounced scrimp. Mrs. Harriet helped me with common phrases as well, such as instead of saying "roads," which is what we had in the South, I should say "street" as the roads here are paved with concrete. Instead of saying, "I have plaits in my hair." I would now use the word "braids" instead. "Over there" replaced "over yonder. "About to" replaced "fitting nah." Want to and going to" replaced "wanna and gonna"; "sneakers" replaced "tennis shoes," and "toilet" replaced "commode." "Y'all" was not considered a word. The most appropriate way to address many people was to say "you."

My Bronxdale Houses pal Asia and I were still friends, and now we walked to school together by ourselves; our school was just across the bridge. We had countless discussions during these times. There were also some embarrassing moments we experienced on our walks as well. One day a bird pooped in her hair. Another time right in front of the school on a snowy day, I slipped on ice and went down in slow motion right in front of the boy I had the biggest crush on, Chase. I was so embarrassed. Even though he didn't know me or my feelings for him, I really didn't want my fall to be the first memory he had of me. When we finally officially met, it turned out that he hadn't seen me sprawled on the ground, struggling to get up while many around me got their laughs on.

Chase. He was very "popular" among the students as well as the teachers because he was a problematic student. He had been in the school for a year already. He had a hot temper, but when he and I spoke, he was very different.

We had many classes together. And the classmates in whom I had confided my feelings for him immediately started making it obvious when he came around, teasing me until he got the message. Now that he knew I liked him, numbers were exchanged. We would talk every night for hours. He made my days at school worth going every day.

My grandmother's work schedule as a health home aide had changed to the afternoon and evening shift. I was to make sure my and my brother's homework was done. She would prepare a meal for us to eat before she went to work. I knew better than to have anyone in the house when she was not there.

That year, for Christmas, Chase gave me a card and a picture of himself. Funny, I still have that picture today. It was the start of a great friendship.

All the while that I was getting to know my classmates, friends from my block and my first crush, I made no mention of the tragedy. I wanted a normal life and gave no signs of how broken I was. I dealt with that life-changing experience and adjustment behind closed doors, crying often and venting on paper. After realizing that crying and venting didn't change anything, I began to pretend things were as they had been when things were perfect in my eyes. Other kids were lucky to have their mothers. I wanted a sense of the same. It was like there was a light switch that I turned on when I was home in my comfort zone and could wallow in my sorrow. Turning the light on showed who I really was. When at school, I turned the light off and began my act. In the dark, not much could be seen. I was very careful to not confuse my dark and light moments.

In my dreams, the most vulnerable moments where I am at my weakest, was when the enemy would strike. My nightmares often woke me up in cold sweats and feeling physically drained as if I had been running. The face of the man who killed my mom and stabbed me appears clear as day in my nightmares. Him coming back to finish what he started. That thought lives in my mind. In the dream, I am often running to get away from danger. Making it a point to run in the opposite direction of family and friends so I would not put anyone else at risk and harm of danger. Then I recalled in one of the dreams, I had made an effort to call someone for help. When I woke up, I felt different. Not as scared. In fact, I had taken strides to help myself.

My grandmother had me attend counseling sessions. However, I didn't want to share my feelings. I was not ready to talk about what I had witnessed. When crying, sulking and pretending did not work, I got involved in many school activities and events to keep my mind off things. It became much easier to smile to cover my pains or smile to keep people from asking questions I had no desire to answer. Although, I was haunted every other night with nightmares, I really enjoyed the way I felt when I did not have to talk or think about it. I not only started believing it, it started to become a part of me and felt real. I became a part of any activity that kept me busy and gave me little time to reminisce.

DEEPER LEVELS OF HELL

Things had truly taken a turn for the worst when one day my grandma began talking about "the light" and "ghost" shining on us from outside and from which she had to protect us. She threw everything in our apartment away. Old and new. We were now sleeping on the floor. She stuck white contact paper on the windows to prevent any light from shining in. She also placed some weird fabrics on the wall in places where the light managed to shine through the contact paper. Our phone had been disconnected and our lights would have to stay turned off. My family had gotten together to find out what could be done to help her because she was clearly losing her mind. My grandmother's youngest sister, Marie, had reached out to a witch doctor and was told someone had a spell on her. We were advised to walk with a bag of garlic in our pocket or anywhere on our person while in our house. This was to kill the spirit.

That familiar moment of living in the shelter, sleeping on the floor or on cots and around strangers, had come to pay us a visit.

My grandma had stopped working and her boyfriend was no longer in the picture. They say an idle mind is the devil's playground. She had fallen into a depressed state, and as the days and years went by, she became no longer fit to care for us.

Her behaviors started to change for the worst. She started drinking and smoking again. There were nights when we had no food and were forced to hang out at a friend's house to get a meal before bed. Uncle Marvin would go out during the day to sell bottles and cans and would often bring home a cinnamon bun for us to eat. Some nights that was all we had. Grandma started giving me $50 in food stamps at the beginning of every month to get food and snacks for my brother and me to last the month.

I had just entered eighth grade and because of the situations taking place at home, I was always anxious to get out of that environment and into one where I could just zone out and be happy. My brother and I made it a point to be at school every day to eat breakfast and lunch considering the limited amount of money we had for the month to eat. We were fortunate to get free lunch tickets in school. The food wasn't the greatest, but there was no other real choice in the matter.

Due to my situations at home, I did not feel comfortable inviting anyone over. However, that did not stop them from coming to my house to peek in and make fun of me for all that we did not have. Kids were and are still so cruel. I wish I had known what I knew today because they would not be called friends. Nor would I have allowed it to bother me because I didn't have control of the situation.

My grandmother started to slowly refurnish the apartment again, but with items from the garbage piles on the block. She would sometimes wait for us to get home and ask us to help drag inside whatever it is she wanted from the garbage pile. It was the most embarrassing duty. The garbage area was in the middle of the cul de sac on the grounds of the projects. My grandmother did not play either. She was quick-tempered and always ready to hit you with anything she could grab. She would call up to our window for us to come down to help her. We would take our time to try to avoid bumping into our friends.

Most of my friends wore the best outfits. We wore all the bottom-of-the-barrel clothes and hand-me-downs. Even if shoes didn't fit, we had to wear them because there were no other options. Grandma would at times find clothes and coats for us to wear in the garbage. I thought I was styling. I went to school one day with the Shearling coat she had found for me. Everyone laughed because it was an old-school version. Something Romie Rome would have worn in the Martin Lawrence sitcom. This was at the time when Chase, the boy I had a crush on, was now giving me attention when he was at school and not suspended. I was very particular about the outfits I would wear so as to not draw attention to myself. At this time, the Reebok 54.11 sneaker was popular. They were called 54.11s because of the price. I wanted a pair so bad, but Grandma said that was just entirely too much money. So I opted to choose a pair that was purple and suede off the table for $20. I didn't want to cause any havoc with my grandma, so I often kept quiet and worked with what we had. Many times I would just settle for dress shoes from Payless. This made it easier to not have to feel that I wasn't keeping up with what everyone else had. I would create my own styles. It's similar to how I live today. I don't try to or make it a point to keep up with every changing style because my attire doesn't define me. If it catches my eye, then I will get it. I guess not having what I wanted shaped that part of me as an adult. I can now say that I am appreciative for that experience.

Much of my early teenage summers were spent in Harlem at my Aunt Mira's house. Aunt Mira would school me on life. She would also show me how to take care of myself as a young lady and how to keep a house clean. I remember one day I came out of the bathroom after a short bath and she sent me right back in to soak. She said I was too light to have crusty elbows and knees. She gave me a rock and told me to scrub. I am conscious of how my skin looks today and take the time to touch on all 2,000 of my parts at least twice. With Aunt Mira, I also remember her making mention of how some light-skinned women carry themselves. She said because most are beautiful or the attention is usually paid to them regardless, they tend to not focus on the obvious. They are so much into their looks that most overlook the most important things, such as hygiene and education. It is funny the advice we remember and refer to as we become of age. I always make it a point to be on top of my hygiene because if I can smell me than others can. Not having the stigma of just being a pretty face and not being able to hold an intellectual conversation is what I have worked hard for through consistently improving my knowledge through education or learning from life experiences.

There was a conversation I overheard between my mother and Aunt Mira right before Mommy passed away that we eventually spoke about. Mommy had asked that if anything happened to her, if my aunt would promise not to let Grandma Meena take us or end up in New York, where Grandma Meena, her sisters and their children were living at the time. Considering my aunt's present situation of having a small child to care for and not having any financial help, that promise could not be kept. However, she dedicated a great deal of her time supporting me in my decision-making and giving me tips on how to be a successful young lady. She was my rock and biggest cheerleader.

I remember the first day I got my period. I remember it like it was yesterday. I was at her house, and after teasing me and having a good laugh, she gave me a pad. My period lasted for a week, but did not return until the same month the following year. We had long talks about dating and sex. It was very uncomfortable to share my thoughts with her on sex no matter how easy and safe she tried to make it. She always addressed me as her 9-month-old baby girl. If I had just gotten my hair washed and blown out, she would ask me to shake it to remind her of when I was little and jumping on the bed with my hair all over the place. I took it all in stride and made it a point not to disappoint her.

It wasn't long before Aunt Mira, her boyfriend and the kids had moved to the Bronx on Tremont. The move made it more convenient for us because now we could walk to her house.

My weekends were the time I could escape the day-to-day drama in my house. It was getting harder to manage $50 a month for food, so I had to find ways to make some extra money to make sure I was holding up my end of the bargain of taking care of my little brother as my mother had asked. I started babysitting, braiding hair and tutoring to make some extra cash. There was now enough money to eat as well as buy new clothing or shoes that we needed for the rest of the school year.

That upcoming summer I was turning 14 and was able to get my working papers. I had attended this job-for-youth program with my cousin Janet. It was there that I learned about entrepreneurship and how to become one. I chose to sell boxer shorts to people I knew in order to get my certificate. It was a really good experience. I was then offered a job as a receptionist in SoHo. This was an awesome experience as I met many people working at the front desk. Although my time there was short, it gave me an introduction of what was expected of me in the world of work.

My grandmother said I needed to get everything required for school with my summer youth checks. It was not much and I knew the money would not stretch that far, but I made the best of it. I still had my job of braiding hair throughout the summer, and once school resumed, I would be able to still tutor.

My aunt Deidre arrived in New York from South Carolina with my little cousin Nikkia after her marriage failed, and she found an apartment in Harlem as well. Although I was older, I still did not feel all that comfortable being around her as a result of her having touched me when I was a kid. Just like with everything else, I pretended nothing happened so I would not have to revisit one of the most uncomfortable moments in my life. I limited my time spent around her. She was all over the place mentally and emotionally. I would babysit Nikkia when Aunt Deidre needed to go out. While at Aunt Deidre's house, I was able to talk to my crush longer. That was my motive for babysitting for her. We still did not have a phone in our house because Grandma would say someone was listening in on our calls and watching us. To talk to my crush, there were many nights I would dress as warmly as I could and call him from a pay phone next to my building and have him call me back on that phone. We would talk until my curfew.

My ninth-grade senior year of junior high school was my most memorable. I was no longer the one everyone teased and made fun of. I was the one who most wanted to be around. I was a tomboy. And I wrestled with the boys every time they would tease me. It was years later, that a few of the boys, now men, confessed their true feelings for me. The special interest my teachers took in me over the years had never changed. If they saw me mingling with someone they felt would be detrimental to my learning, they would pull me aside to make sure I knew better. Mr. Norbit was my social studies teacher. He wanted us students to succeed and did not tolerate nonsense. I truly understand today how difficult it is to get and keep the attention of an entire class. Teachers are responsible for teaching the materials to achieve or perform well on tests. However, they are not responsible for the knowledge obtained.

There was also Mrs. K. She was my health teacher. In or out of class, she would always take the time to answer my questions about sex or my body. Questions I didn't feel comfortable talking to my aunt Mira about. She walked me through putting on a tampon and gave me key pointers on when it was safe times to have sex. Before or immediately following my period when there was no egg available. And of course, using protection always. Rules that have stuck with me, and by which I currently live. It's funny how I am not even in a sexual mood during the unsafe weeks.

While in school, my crush, Chase, was extremely overprotective and short-tempered. Which in my young age, found to be cute. No other boy could be near me. One day, we were in Spanish class and my good friend Malik was sitting next to me as he usually did. Chase walked in and saw him sitting next to me and went ballistic. He asked Malik why he was sitting next to me. When Malik replied, "Because I wanted to," Chase went crazy. He picked up a chair and threw it in his direction then growled like he was the Incredible Hulk. They fought until security came in. Chase was suspended.

I was not happy about his suspension because that meant I would not see him for a while. I decided to go over to his house to visit him after school one day to check on him. I knocked on his door and his father said he was not in.

Chase had been what I used as motivation to get me through my days. To keep me emotionally balanced with other pains I was feeling. It had been now two years of us talking and getting to know each other. He always made it a point to give me his full attention when I was in his presence. He was not only my first crush, overtime, he became my first love. The one I gave my virginity to. The feeling that I had for this boy was one that could not be explained. I would just smile. I walked around with his picture in my wallet just to have him near. I needed glasses because my vision was shot, but even from far distances I could always see him. He was my kryptonite. He became my friend and protector. I was in so deep. To me, he was the right person and it was the right time to give myself to him. Today, I absolutely have no regrets, even though our time together was short.

When I was 14, my grandmother was so paranoid about me getting pregnant early like my mom. She took me to the doctor and insisted that I be checked to make sure I was still a virgin and to request birth control pills for me. The doctor and I spoke, and once I told him that I was not sexually active, he didn't do an exam. However, to appease my grandmother, he did prescribe me the pills. She would be on me to take them every day, but because I knew I was not doing anything, I would toss them out the window.

At school, we had health and sex education classes that gave me the information necessary to make the best decisions. That was more helpful than my grandmother's "If you have sex and get pregnant, Imma kill you" speech. The way in which she introduced the topic to me sparked my curiosity. I was a tomboy and often hung out with the boys. One day, I was sitting outside on the bench talking to one of my homeboys and she came outside looking for me. It was broad daylight and she was breaking, threatening to hurt him if she ever caught him talking to me again. All the measures she went through to prevent me from having sex with her threats did not prevent it from happening; it made me more curious to try it. I just moved smarter for her not to find out.

When I lost my virginity and made love to the love of my life for the very first time, it was after trying three different times. The third time was a charm. He was so gentle and understanding, during the times it didn't happen. He would just hold me and we would talk. Straight out of a movie. Because we spent so much time together and most of the time just chilling, many thought it happened much earlier than it actually did. I was his first and he was mine.

The experience of losing my virginity with whom I lost it with meant a lot and has stamped my heart forever.

In hindsight, it seems I was verbally given the tools necessary to make better decisions but what seemed normal to me and what my heart desired came from actions and situations witnessed. There was clearly a disconnect between my mental and emotional self.

Through the years, he and I have reconnected many times and remained really good friends. One day someone he knew asked us how it felt after all these years to be reconnected with our first love and maybe have the option to rekindle? There was even a time when he had asked me to travel with him and his family to Virginia to spend time. I even attended church with them here in New York. When we went to Virginia, before going to the room that he was to sleep in, he would come in to mine and keep me company, just talking until I fell asleep. No hanky panky was going at this time, and definitely not under his parents' roof. I was older, entering my 20s and knew better. It gave us that much more time to learn more about each other. We would just walk and talk. If we had pursued a relationship when we didn't know any better, we may not have been able to appreciate the moments we have shared today. He surprised me on my last birthday with a picture of us from eighth grade in a frame that read "Live, Love, Laugh" and a bottle of white zinfandel. He knows me well. Sweet and white is what I prefer. It was the most thoughtful and sentimental gift. He knows me and my likes and that made the difference. We never know what life holds for us, but a lifelong friendship can mean so much more than taking chances ruining it with a relationship.

But as children, Chase was a huge piece of what kept me from that dark place that I knew all too well. There were many activities I took part in to stay focused. Ending my elementary years and beginning my junior high school years, I took part in talent shows and school plays. I played the flute and participated in African American fashion shows. Outside school, I played with some of the girls that I met during my first couple of months living at Bronxdale: Renea, Dasia, Maria, Lisa, Kim and Brianna were their names. We would play in the back park of our building. We were either out on the benches talking, or running around playing hide and seek, catch and kiss or skellzies (tops). One summer, boxing gloves were brought out for us to challenge one another. We also enjoyed bike riding or playing dominos with the older women. Then there was football in the big grassy area in the back park with the boys in the winter months.

Bike riding was the best. Dasia was big on riding as a form of exercise. She always stayed active. If she was not walking far, her bike was always ready to be ridden.

So I bought a bike and we would take long rides outside of Bronxdale. I made it a point to make visits across the bridge to see Chase as well. One day we were on our way back from McDonald's. I thought I was the bomb riding with one hand and holding my food in the other. I had my hand on the front break and someone threw a crate in front of me and I hit the break and flipped over. I didn't realize hitting the front break wasn't the smartest idea. The food was in one piece. I walked away pissed with a cut on my thigh. We made the best of our summer months.

It was time for high school, and I wasn't sure what school I wanted to attend; I did not have an interest in anything specific. So like everybody else, I just applied to many schools. I was accepted to Grace Dodge High School. My junior high school ended in ninth grade, so I entered Dodge as a tenth-grader. There was an overwhelmingly number of girls. And it felt like only about 20 boys attended. A couple of the girls at my new school looked and dressed like boys, with bandannas and their hair in cornrows braided in straight rows from front to back and in full, baggy attire. They would stare me down and follow me to class, which made me uncomfortable. I couldn't get with the environment at all and I imagined many fights in the near future. It seems that in all my years of growing up, I have gravitated to the male of our species. It was quite uncomfortable to have females in my space. I felt awkward around them. I didn't play the touchy-feely games. I barely hugged women unless it was a case of showing empathy or maybe in greeting. There are some demons you can't escape. Being touched inappropriately for quite some time by a woman has conditioned my mind to shy completely away from such interactions.

I knew that if I wasn't happy with my high school choice, I could transfer into my zoned school. So I had a talk with Grandma. I would at times only go to school for homeroom and to attend only the classes I wanted. Then I would go home to watch soap operas.

She didn't know my schedule and thought that I was out for the day. When the cut slips started coming in, I would be the one to get them in the mail. I knew she would eventually find out, so I sat my grandmother down and sold her on a plan that I wasn't sure would work, but that I was willing to try just so I wouldn't have to be in that school anymore. I told her the zoned school, Stevenson, was closer to home and I would be able to get a job in the area where it was located because there was a shopping mall nearby. She agreed to complete the paperwork for my transfer. I had made a deal and was determined to make it work.

My first year at Adlai E. Stevenson High School was a breeze because the workload was familiar and most of my longtime classmates from elementary and junior high school went to Stevenson. High school was set up to make or break you for adulthood. There was a greater sense of freedom in high school, but it all depended on you.
My high school experience was nothing like my junior high experience. It was more business-oriented. Like the real world. I wasn't able to be involved in any school activities due to my need to work and take care of my brother and myself.

In my second year, I learned of this co-op work program. It was the perfect opportunity to work and go to school. I applied, and was accepted. I would work one week and go to school the next week for the entire school year. The way the classes were scheduled was like being in junior high school all over again. Everyone chosen for this program would follow the same academic track.

I worked at Ernst & Young, an accounting firm in the city. I was an assistant in the tax library. I learned data entry and got a brief introduction to Lotus notes. The department was in serious need of help getting things prepared for tax season. I remember my co-workers Stella, Bernadette and Kim. They were peas in the pod. Stella was my entertainment, Bernadette was like the parent and Kim stayed to herself, but was always ready to teach me something new.

It was a very comfortable learning environment. When I learned it was just for the season, I was really sad and it broke my heart to leave this location once everything was set. Although I learned early on that nothing is life last forever, it was still hard to wrap my head around it all and accept it. They planned a nice going-away party for me. The office staff gave me a brown leather backpack as a gift; one I still have and use for school today.

Bernadette took me out for lunch one day and introduced me to eggplant parmesan. The only pasta I had ever tasted up until that point was spaghetti. Eggplant parmesan was definitely an acquired taste. I was appreciative of the introduction and experience. I made it a point to try other pasta dishes soon after. Kim was Korean and would bring home-cooked dishes for us to try. She also introduced me to the beef jerky from her country. I quickly became addicted to it.

One of my best qualities, looking back over my life, is that I was always open-minded and eager not only for family love and affection, but information and knowledge also. I was never too proud, self-centered or antisocial to learn or gain as I moved through life.

I was placed in two other departments doing light clerical and secretarial work. Longtime friendships came from these work experiences. I stayed the remainder of my second year in high school through the summer until the program was ended altogether. The wheels were turning in planning for my next job.

In the meantime, my brother had been getting in and out of trouble in the streets. He had decided to drop out of school when my grandmother told him if he couldn't do well in school, he might as well get a job. There was no persuading him to stay in school. He opted to take what he thought was the easy road and dropped out. Soon after, he got caught up with the streets and drugs.

As for me, there were new department stores opening across the street from my high school, so I made it a point to apply to all of them. Danice Fashions, Jimmy Jazz, Old Navy and Pergament

Home Center were the new stores built. I had my heart set on Pergament Home Center and was hoping they would call. It was a huge home improvement store. It seemed to be a company where I could really learn and grow.
It's something about big, well-known companies that peak my interest.

Instead, it was Danice Fashions $10 store that called me for a job. I accepted the job because time was winding down and I knew I couldn't be out of work. But the first day was enough for me. I was responsible for putting all the clothes on hangers. Management was rude and disrespectful. I took my lunch break and never came back. It wasn't a good fit. I didn't feel comfortable or that I belonged there.

Aunt Mira called to find out how the new job was going. She had walked with me to each of the stores to complete the applications. I told her where my heart was but that I had given Danice a shot because of my need. Then, a couple of days later, Pergament Home Center called to offer me a job. I was too happy that my prayers were answered. When I went in to start, it felt like I belonged. It became my new home away from home for the next four years, and was where I bonded with many people (associates and customers) who are longtime friends today, and was a place where I was coached and promoted not too long after arriving. I started as a sales associate in the wallpaper department, and after a little over two years, I was made the supervisor. I had many great experiences there and made what I thought at that time was good money. I was making a little above minimum wage as well as commission for the window treatments we were selling. I had a supervisor that looked like an older version of me. Yvette Foley was her name. She was very stern. I have always been well disciplined and well mannered, so working with her was a piece of cake. Others couldn't understand our relationship.

In the South, the saying 'It takes a village to raise a child,' is so true and they take it seriously. If a neighbor saw me doing something out of line, I would get my first tongue lashing from him or her, and before I got home, my mother would have already heard about it and a whipping was in tow. I would never forget my elementary school teacher Ms. Welfaro. Not sure of the year I had her, but she had permission from my mother to paddle me if I got out of line. My momma didn't play; if she had to come to school for any reason, I would get it in school also.

My grandmother was different. I remember getting a D on my report card for not turning in my homework. I knew it was scored wrong, and thought I would have a hard time getting my grandmother to believe me, but to my surprise, she came with me to school the next day and threatened the teacher. Told her if she weren't able to prove to her that my homework wasn't turned in and right her wrong, she would put her head through the blackboard. I am not saying it was right but it felt good for her to believe and defend me. My grandmother goes a little far with it though because even when there is grounds and evidence she will still say, "Oh no, not mine."

At Pergament, most thought Yvette Foley was mean, but from dealing with my grandmother and growing up with tough love, I thought she was sweet. She was rather tough on some of my co-workers, but for good reason. Most would come in late, or while on the job, would not be doing what they were paid to do. She was like a mother to me. Her husband, Woody, also worked at Pergament, as the supervisor of electrical. Together they were the perfect couple and surrogate parents. I realize now how lucky I was to have them both. They took a serious interest in my life and education. I bumped into her some years back, six years after she had left Pergament, and to my surprise, she had my picture that I had given her in her wallet. It was so touching.

If not your own kin, there are often others who will take a serious interest in you and can fill voids if you're open and allow them to. Although I didn't understand it then, I truly understand its effects today.

Meanwhile, I was trying to maintain balance at school and work as drama increased at home. My brother and I were sharing a room. I had gotten a personal fridge, a computer and a phone line in our room. My grandmother had now asked that I start contributing money toward rent. I was reluctant given that I also had to make sure my brother was taken care of, but to keep the peace, I obliged. Her behavior was increasingly getting out of control. At times, she would come in my room in the wee hours of the morning and snoop around hoping to find money. When she couldn't find my stash, she would wake me up asking for money. If she didn't get what she was asking for, she went crazy and starting spazing out. Lights were flipped on and the volume of her voice grew. I knew what was next. She would ask me to leave, no matter what time of the night or morning. There were days I would give her what she asked for just to get a good night's sleep. Then there were other days I truly didn't have it. This was in addition to having to give her my share of rent for the month. Those days I was put out in the street. It was the absolute scariest feeling because nine times out of ten, it was after midnight. Trouble and evil lurk in those hours. I would reach out to friends hoping to just get through the rest of the night until work or school. I found myself calling men that I knew that had their own places to crash for the night. I had no physical interest and having sex wasn't an option or on the table so I didn't make it a habit. At times, if my brother were there we would just go in the back park of the building and sit on the bench and wait until the sun came up.

God was truly steering the wheel in those years because giving up wasn't an option. However, the hand dealt seemed to be a set up to fail. Being forced into the streets of the darkest, the unknown to fend for self or get what's needed from strangers and strays could've opened up doors that may have seemed appealing at the time, but I didn't walk through them.

Upon reaching my senior year of high school, my supervisor moved on and the torch was passed to me. The opportunity to show and prove is the greatest gift at times, and all you have to give in return is your all. Not a bad trade-off.
I had a staff of four. Learning to be a supervisor to people who were once my peers was hard. You would think they would respect the position because of the relationship that had already been established. Instead, they chose to take advantage of situations and

had to be reprimanded. Enemies were made because at the end of the day, I had a job to do and responsibilities.

Yvette Foley had trained me well, and taking over the department was a great experience. I also was paid more money, which meant I would be able to afford my upcoming senior expenses without setting me back regarding the money I needed to pay Grandma for rent or to take care of my brother. Although he wasn't in school and went in and out of jail, I still felt it was my responsibility to make sure he was good.

I got along very well with everyone at Pergament. Willie, one of my managers, was someone in particular with whom I had opened up and shared some things that I was going through. He walked in my office one day when I had taken a moment to just have a good cry. He closed the door, and for the first time, I poured it all out to him. My struggles and woes, the things I was going through in my house that I had no control over. He sympathized and asked if there was anything he could do. And overtime, he simply started arriving to open the store earlier than usual so that I could do homework or rest on those nights I would get kicked out. This helped tremendously.

My aunt Deidre had lost her apartment and had now moved in with us. Our apartment was very crowded. I had offered to have my little cousin Nikkia sleep in my room with me. My aunt and uncle slept in the living room. My uncle Marvin still lived with us too, but he was up and out very early to do his recycling, and often didn't come back until very late.

Nikkia was now completing her last month at the same elementary school that my brother had attended and was preparing to go junior high school. Rather than come to my bedroom to sleep, Nikkia preferred to sleep on the couch just to be in her mother's arms. My aunt had managed to meet friends in the area quickly, and she began sneaking out in the middle of the night when Nikkia had fallen asleep and not making it back in time to get things together for her to go school. So, before I left for work, I would get Nikkia up and out. For school, I was her emergency contact and for what it was worth, assumed full responsibility for her. I made sure she did her homework and that she had food to eat daily.

Grandma started getting drunk and violent more frequently. She had a boyfriend who would come over to spend time with her. When she was intoxicated, there was almost always a fight that broke out between the two of them.

One morning, I woke up to blood running down the hallway walls as if someone had been bleeding and struggled to balance while trying to get out of the apartment. I walked into my grandmother's room and there she was in her nightgown all bloody and in a daze because she could not remember what had happened. Days later, her boyfriend came back with a big gash in his head and with the police. We were in the back park when they approached my grandmother. He was so scared to tell what had happened, she just attacked him verbally in front of the police. They asked him if she had done anything to him. He could not say yes in front of the cops. She told him to stop wasting the police officers' time, grabbed his arm and told him it was time to go upstairs. He agreed and we all went upstairs.

I never understood relationships that were based around violence and where both people claimed to be in love. While her boyfriend was in our house, she would lay off me, but the moment he would leave, I was her target again. I made it a point to insist that Nikkia sleep in my room every night. I didn't want anything to happen to her while out in the living room asleep. My biggest concern was her witnessing an act of violence that could change her life forever such as what had happened to me.

My high school years seemed to have gone by so fast. I met a good friend of mine named Monica. She was a sweetheart and what was most admirable was that she was very close to her mom. A sense of jealousy always came over me when I saw girls with their mothers. It warmed my heart to be in the presence of them both. She lived right across the street from the job and our school. We had a few classes together. She even started working at Pergament as well. As the end of the year approached we grew closer. At the last minute, we got together and planned to rent a limo for senior prom night and had a blast.

On prom night, our first stop was Marina del Ray. We then had to make it downtown for the after party, which was a boat ride around the Statue of Liberty. Our final destination was the Step In restaurant in the Parkchester section of the Bronx for breakfast.

That night, I was introduced to a guy named David who became my boyfriend for two years and a longtime friend.

Step In restaurant seemed to have been the spot for everyone. We had a good breakfast surrounded by a few of the guys from our school. This had to have been the most memorable experience of high school. At graduation, David, the guy I met at the prom, was caught staring in amazement behind me in one of my pictures. He introduced himself again. He was sweet and seemed harmless. He pulled me in with his silliness and sense of humor. We exchanged numbers and hit it off quick on the phone. He would come to pick me up with his little brother Aaron that I love so dearly still to this day. Interestingly enough, he was born on May 5. The day that was an anniversary for something unforgettable and tragic in my life had been given additional meaning. The original meaning was never to be forgotten. However, it was one less day to possibly experience an emotional relapse. A celebration of life now was on tap for that day.

We spent a lot of time together and he finally popped the question: "Would you be my girlfriend?" I took him up on it. He introduced me to his family within days and I felt the warmth immediately. Introducing him to the world I was not too proud of was not an option. I told him about all that I was going through, so most of our time was spent outdoors dining out, hanging on the grounds of the Parkchester residential complex, partying or at his house. He played basketball and I made sure I was at every game to support him. He became my best friend and my escape.

After graduating from Stevenson High School, I was uncertain of what I wanted to do in life. I had taken accounting and business classes in high school, along with my work experience, but none of it excited me. I knew I was going to attend college, but wasn't sure where. I knew I couldn't go far because I didn't want to leave my brother. Going away wasn't an option. I got accepted to a technical college and had to come up with $2,000. I still had no idea what would interest me, but I had five months to figure it out and get the funds up. So I decided to take a vacation and go see my Grandma Flore in South Carolina. I knew that there was a very big chance I would see my father, and seeing him would be bittersweet.

A SLICE OF FAMILIARITY AND HAPPINESS

I hadn't seen Grandma Flore since the Christmas before my mom passed away and I hadn't seen or heard from my father since the hospital incident. It had left a bad taste in my mouth, but I still needed an explanation as to why he left us. Did he not want us? Looking back on it now, I realize he was a coward. The least he could have given us was time or a consistent phone call once a day, considering that someone else was taking care of us.

I read his name in the guest book for Mommy's funeral but he didn't make it a point to look for us. The next time I saw him wasn't until I turned 18years old after high school graduation.

When I was 13years old, I went to visit some childhood friends who live in Orangeburg, South Carolina, but had moved from Edisto Drive. One day, I decided to look up my father's mother, Grandma Flore, in the phone book and call her. I was nervous, but wanted so badly to be reunited with my family that I knew. She lived in Charleston, South Carolina. Every Christmas, they would send for us and it was where we spent our holidays. To my surprise, my grandma's number and voice was the same. It was refreshing for both of us to speak to each other. By that time, it had been four years of no contact.

We spent a lot of time on the phone together from that moment until her last breath, which took place right after my daughter was born. We had a beautiful relationship. She was a widow with six children. My father being the oldest, and her one daughter, who was the youngest.

After sharing with Grandma Meena that I had reached out to my father's family, she went ballistic. In an effort to protect us from our past, she didn't share our whereabouts with anyone and had very little contact with anyone from the South. Many times when I would call Great-grandma Ann when my grandma wanted to speak to her mom, I would use the star-67 function so that the phone number would be blocked and it would come up in caller ID as a private call.

But after contacting Grandma Flore, she became a huge part of our lives again. She picked up where she left off. She started sending money when she could, which helped especially when it was time for senior dues and activities.

So after my senior graduation, I was looking forward to seeing her and that side of my family again. This reunion was overdue and it felt good to visit the better parts of my past. My brother and I took a Greyhound bus down to Charleston. Everything was as I remembered it. The house was still in the same location and beautiful. Grandma had aged but basically still looked the same. When we arrived she was sitting in her favorite spot on the sofa in the living room. Unfortunately, she had fallen ill and had been diagnosed with diabetes. She had had to have her toes amputated by this time and was losing her sight. We spent a week there.

My aunt, my father's sister, took us around to see various members of the family. Having experienced death many times up until this point, it saddened me to know that Grandma Flore would become too sick and death would be knocking. Through it all, Grandma was still active. We would take walks around the block and make runs to the supermarket and bank.

It has always been hard for me to be around the sick. I remember when I was little my aunt Faye was very sick and Grandma Meena would take me with her when she would go to help her. I would insist on sitting on the porch and didn't mind waiting out by myself. The sick also always had a scent.

So, when I learned that Grandma Flore was as ill as she was, I had to prepare myself for the stay. As night fell and Grandma told us where we would be sleeping, I grew a bit disturbed. She told me I would be sleeping with her. I imagined her foot would somehow touch me, keeping me up half the night. So I planned to take a quick nap and wake up before everyone and surprise them with breakfast. Grandma beat me to it. I was sound asleep and did not realize my grandmother's movement from the bed. She was amazing. Sleeping with Grandma was not as bad as I thought it would be. I loved her dearly.

Throughout our time there, we visited my uncles and friends of the family who remembered us when we were younger. Everyone dug in their pockets to give us money for the many years lost. That Southern family love and generosity. I managed to collect $1,500 of the $2,000 needed for college. All but my father managed to have come around and spend time with us until it was time for our return home to the Big Apple. It was a beautiful stay. I always get emotional when leaving a place or people I love. I cried so hard.

As we were pulling out of the bus station, we heard someone running and screaming after the bus. The man managed to get the attention of the bus driver, who stopped the bus and conversed with the gentleman for a few seconds before calling out for my brother and me. As we walked to the front of the bus, we noticed that the man who had been so desperately running down the bus was our father, Andrew.

He looked exactly as I had remembered him. He began to say how sorry he was not coming to see us sooner. It truly didn't make sense; there was always an excuse. In the car that he had ridden to the bus station, there were many people and he made it a point to introduce us. We heard many comments of how well we had grown and how good we looked. He stood with a smile as the proud father he wasn't. The bus driver honked, signaling our time was up. My brother was so angry, he didn't say hello or goodbye to our father. He just walked back on the bus. I, unlike my brother, wanted some goodbye affection from my dad. My father was always a disappointment to us, so we had grown to expect it, but for some reason it was hard to accept it and move on. I wanted a daddy.

There was a serious void and a need to be love and accepted by the one parent who was alive, but after many years, and finally getting to express my feelings to him, I have grown to accept it.

As the years went by, I continued to keep in touch. It felt good to be connected to the family that I had been around while Mommy was alive. The feelings took me back to the moments in time when life was normal.

I arrived back in New York with a plan to attend Berkley College. I started the paperwork process and impulsively put the money down. After reading the fine print, I realized how much more money I would need as the years went on and I grew uninterested. I started getting responses from the CUNY schools I applied to, and I decided to attend Lehman College, where I did my undergraduate studies in computing and management on full financial aid. With my income and no parents, the aid was certainly a blessing.

Looking back, I regret deciding to stay in the city and attend school there. Not so much for the experience of being on my own, but being able to focus on myself and have peace of mind. The experience of being on my own, paying bills and taking care of myself was forced upon me early. So I wasn't missing anything in that area. However, learning to share space with another in a dorm or having meet-up groups to study, learn new things and build a group of college friends for life would've been beneficial to my journey. I am weak in those areas. Living with someone will be a challenge. Most of my studying and gathering information for projects is done alone. I do well on a team, but I suck at sharing duties or delegating because I don't trust anyone and prefer to do it myself.

WHEN HOME IS NO REFUGE

I was quickly finding out what kind of drama would transpire as a result of Aunt Deidre's moving in with us. I still felt a lot of animosity toward Aunt Deidre because of what she had done to me as a kid, so we never really got along.

The most conversation we had concerned what was going on with her daughter, Nikkia, and school. She had no interest.

But I wasn't home enough to concern myself with the lifestyle and behavior of everyone in my household.
There were times I came in late and would sit in the living room, if Aunt Deidre or my uncle weren't there, to do my homework on my typewriter and avoid distracting my cousin Nikkia. I kept my other electronics locked away in my room along with my file cabinet and safe, which secured my most personal items. But my brother was usually home to let Nikkia in so that she could do her homework and grab food from my fridge.

Then, one night, my aunt Deidre robbed us and tried to make it seem like someone else did it by leaving the door wide open. I was a fool to leave my typewriter in the living room, but not fool enough to believe what she said about someone else robbing us.

We had woken up and noticed the door ajar. We then looked around and realized my typewriter was gone. Oddly enough, there was my grandmother's stereo, TV and VCR still sitting near where my typewriter had been.

My grandmother believed that crap from my aunt because that was her baby girl and she did no wrong in her eyes. But word around the block was that she was exchanging any and everything with any value for drugs. A drug dealer told me. I was pissed and wanted to go to war. The tension in the house was high.

The thefts continued. I came home one day and my stereo had been stolen, file cabinet broken into and my safe banged up. My grandmother said my aunt was in need and that I hadn't been home for her to ask me. We argued, and from then on, because she had broken the lock on my door, she would come in and search me at night and steal whatever money she could find.

One morning, the police raided our apartment. I was on my way out the door when a squad of police appeared in front my door. I was cornered and questioned. They were looking for drugs. My brother was selling drugs. My aunt was a user. My grandmother smoked weed and my uncle smoked, but was more mentally unstable; his level of aggression due to his not taking his medicine almost got him arrested that day. I had to be at work and I pleaded with the police to let me go. I offered to be drug tested. Police released me and I quickly left the building to head to work. It was a good thing that Nikkia had already left to go to school.

My brother was arrested that day for all the drugs they found. Sadly enough, I didn't know or think drugs would be kept in the room where we slept. Or maybe I just didn't think he would put us both in danger. He was given a smack on the wrist and was out within no time.

My brother's not being home as a supplier seemed to negatively affect the attitudes of everyone in my household. My grandmother was more aggressive about needing money. My aunt was staying out and away from home more often and for longer periods. My uncle started arguing with and putting his hands on my aunt and grandmother at times. Sometimes, he would just look at me and roll his eyes. Then five minutes later, he would make conversation, asking me about my day. He meant well. I starting receiving calls from Nikkia's school, reporting that she had been cutting classes and that I needed to come in and talk to the teacher.

I was just fed up with everyone, but even more frustrated with my brother and Nikkia. It was a huge burden to take care of my little cousin and I was barely home. So, I made the decision to reach out to my aunt's father, Nikkia's grandfather, Bill Wayward.

He and his wife had always been part of Deidre and Nikkia's lives. They were very disappointed with Deidre and would call often to check on them. Over the years, she had taken trips to visit them, and he would call saying she was stealing from him and for me to be careful. The person she had become and the influences she had taken on had affected many. So, he understood the situation and agreed to help me take care of Nikkia. The plan was that he would raise her and I would financially help him. I requested time off from work, purchased our Greyhound tickets and packed her up.

I didn't tell anyone because I knew that neither her mother nor her grandmother would understand the importance of her having a safe home where she would have a chance. I spoke with Nikkia about it and promised that we would talk often and that I would send money for her. She would miss her mom for sure.

When I got back from taking Nikkia to her grandfather, I shared the decision I had made, and to my surprise, Aunt Deidre and Grandma weren't as mad as I expected they would be.

It was a dispute over—what else—money that broke the camel's back regarding my relationship with my aunt Deidre. My brother's friend had begun approaching me as I came in from work, inquiring about my aunt's whereabouts because she owed him money. My aunt had received a settlement check in the amount of $8,000, and she had given me $4,000 of it to hold for her. She and I had agreed on the amounts to send to her father to help care for her daughter, and she finally agreed to replace the items she had stolen from me. But it's unbelievable how much money you can go through when you have a habit you cannot kick. Every, single night she would have me leave an amount of money for her in an envelope somewhere in the house so that when she came in late at night, she would not have to wake me. I warned her about the man who was looking for her. He was threatening to kill her if he didn't get his money. She did everything to avoid him, but she finally agreed to pay him out of the money she had left.

A short time later, my aunt began asking for money, and when I told her she didn't have anymore, she lost her cool. I was getting ready for work one morning and she was screaming and hollering that I had stolen her money and that she couldn't have spent all of that money. It was at that moment that my grandmother came to my defense for the first time in years. She reminded my aunt of all the requests she had made for money and about the money used to pay off the drug dealer. My aunt still wanted to fight. That's when I lost my cool. "If I wanted to take your money I could've," I said. "Hell, I was holding it. I could've did you as dirty as you did me."

I know God doesn't like ugly and karma doesn't discriminate. I never needed to steal or take from anyone to get ahead. I am too blessed. I may not have a lot but I always have what I need and a doorway of opportunity to take advantage of. After getting my point across, I just tuned out my aunt, and she didn't like that. She charged me, and my grandmother jumped in. The rage that I felt would've landed me in jail that day. I told my grandmother to let her go, that I had been waiting for the moment to beat the living hell out of her for years. I was in the bathroom curling my hair and had all intentions of branding her face. Scarring her like she had done me. Violating me when I had had no control or understanding of what she was doing to me. It was from then on that we did not speak.

The madness that took place in my household had its affects. I made it a point to not let my hurt or anger show in my face or attitude, but it began to show up in my school performance. It was getting harder to concentrate. It was a party every night in my house. There were nights hearing things that took place outside of my room that would have distracted and driven a sane person crazy, but not me. This was my life. The arguing, fighting, talking and music playing always rang loud in the air at any given time of the day or night. The madness that went on in my dreams at night was a never-ending battle. The same nightmares that were so vivid, and had me waking up in cold sweats. My grades had dropped trying to juggle everything, and I was put on academic probation. It was a hard pill to swallow, but I had to take time off just to gather myself. I just wanted to get it done and over with.

That was sort of the attitude I had with many things. Just wanting to get things done quickly, sometimes missing out on many points that should have been learned. Aimlessly going through life, lost, with no interests or real desires.

Taking a semester off did do some good. I was able to free my mind and surround myself in different environments where only happiness lived. I was a pleasure and peace-seeker. I was barely home, spending most of my time at my boyfriend's house if I wasn't working or hanging out with my friends Asia and Monica at Parkside Plaza on Fridays and the Tunnel on Sundays.

The devil always knows when to strike. Either in my strongest or weakest moments, it didn't matter to him. I had taken a week off from work to just relax. After I had paid my portion of rent, my grandmother asked for more money. My brother needed carfare and money to take passport pictures for a job, Aunt Deidre needed money to go to welfare for some type of assistance. (I knew that was a lie because she didn't have her daughter or the will to take care of any business.) My uncle needed money for cigarettes and my grandma needed money for her poison. I simply told my grandmother no. I gave my brother what he needed. All seemed fine until early the next morning.

Grandma woke up banging on doors, and screaming for me to get up and that I knew what everyone needed. I simply repeated what I had told her the night before. She grabbed an iron and threw it at me. It just missed my face. She came charging but my brother jumped in to hold her back.

I never thought to put my hands on my grandmother. All the years growing up, she would tell me, as a warning, that the reason my mother died young was because she had disobeyed God and had hit her. Every so often, I would remind my grandmother that I was there when she attacked my mother and all she did was simply defend herself. But although I knew what had happened, I was still afraid of dying young as a punishment if I hit her.

Grandma grabbed my bag and left the apartment. She went down to the payphone to call the cops and told them I had beaten her. I didn't think things would have turned out as bad as they did that day. So I focused on getting dressed and getting out. My aunt told me to leave before my grandmother came back, but before I could, my grandmother came back in. She started punching me in my stomach and kicking me. I grabbed her up to prevent her from hitting me. My aunt and brother were there to break it up, but by that time, the cops were knocking. My grandmother had bruised herself more and told them I had done it. The cops walked me out in cuffs and said I had to find somewhere to go if I did not want to go to jail. I still had on my pajamas and they wouldn't even let me back in the house to get some clothes. I went to my boyfriend's house where I began thinking of my next move.

Later that day, my brother brought me my clothes and books for work and school. He's always had my back. He loves me to pieces and had always been my protector. He would argue with his friends if they tried to compliment me and was ready to confront a man I was dating if things didn't seem right to him. But he was constantly in and out of jail and his attitude had worsened over the years. He walked around with such aggression and was extremely emotional. I had created the expectation that I would always be there for him, which enabled him. There was no cutoff period given or a list of stipulations in this agreement with my mom to always take care of my younger brother.

During this time, my brother had made the decision to go down South to stay with our uncle Moe from our father's side of the family. Soon after his arrival, he got into more trouble with the law. It was said that he had violently beaten someone. He had to serve time.

Nikkia's grandfather and I spoke frequently as I had promised. My little cousin had started giving her grandparents problems displaying similar characteristics of her mother. This was no surprise as she was doing the same when she was here with me. However, I was hopeful that the apple would fall further from the tree being in a different environment. I tried hard to protect her and not have her exposed to the negative toxic acts going on under our roof to give her a chance to be better than me. However, with my obligations of work and school, that was impossible.

DESCENT INTO DEPRESSION

The darkness that resided inside me began to haunt me. For a period of three years, 1999–2001, I lost hope and the will to live. The darkness blurred my vision, stripped me of emotions and took over my thoughts.

Being the chameleon that I am, I was able to mask those feelings while at work. My job was my lifeline. It was the only place where I felt a part of a family or a team, where my existence mattered. Setting my alarm clock to wake up, clocking in and out at work, created a sense of structure. Having to request days off and get approval privileges and the many obligations for which you are responsible as an employee, all made me feel needed and wanted, thus making life much more meaningful to me. Almost like a child to a parent. The world of work was the place where I connected with individuals from different backgrounds, age groups and with various experiences, and it was my escape. I was able to put aside negative thoughts when I was in work mode.

During this period of not being able to be in the home where I grew up and sleep in the bed where I was most comfortable despite the drama, had it effects on me. I stayed some nights at my aunt Mira's house with her and the kids in the Bronx near Gun Hill Road or at my cousin Janet's in the same area, yet I could not get too comfortable.

Drama and violence were what I was used to. I didn't enjoy being in or around it, but it kept me going; it was part of me and what I had been used to for all the years I had been on this earth. Sort of like an abusive relationship. It hurt, but I was comfortable and knew it as being love on some level. So I accepted it.

****

At least once a week, I would return to my grandmother's to get clothes. One day, I walked in to find my uncle stomping my grandmother in the face. I intervened and what came after was not expected. My uncle turned from my grandmother, and without a second's hesitation, swung on me. And a fistfight commenced. My uncle was clearly not in his right mind and I had to protect myself.

There had been times he wouldn't take his medication and would talk and laugh to himself, but never had I thought he was a threat and would hurt me. This was the man who had walked me to elementary school, kept my childhood secrets and gave me a sense of security. I was now fighting for my life with someone who was mentally challenged and didn't recognize me.

I had left the front door to my grandmother's apartment open. So my goal was to lure him toward the door and put him out. I managed to grab him up and as I punched him and pushed him out the door, he grabbed my shirt, ripping it and my bra. Once he was out the door and on the floor, I closed and locked the door and ran to my grandma. I called for an ambulance and the police. Instead of my uncle leaving, he started kicking, banging and screaming through the door. The cops seemed to always come quick. As if they were stationed in the projects ready to respond. They walked up just in time.

My uncle was arrested. Years later, I found out he was placed in a mental institution.

And although my grandmother had turned her back on me for years and given me a hard way to go, I still loved her. I rushed her to the hospital that night after the beating. Her face was swollen and bleeding, which was hard to view and stomach. After spending a few days in the hospital, she came home.

When she found out that her son, who had just assaulted her, had been arrested, she became furious with me. She cursed me out every chance she got for calling the "people," which is what she called the police, on her son and now she didn't know where he was. I was accused and verbally abused for being dependable and taking care of her. Something she knew little about.

Then Aunt Mira, the only person who was there as my gas station to refuel me when needed, had begun to deteriorate; the diagnosis was multiple sclerosis. She fell sick during the mid 1990s. Most didn't think I could handle knowing the truth of the time limit on her life that she had been given, so they opted not to tell me. My aunt was in and out of the hospital—it seemed like every other month—for weeks at a time. I was still feeling traumatized by my hospital stay. So being comfortable whenever I visited her was not something I would ever feel. Because of my fear of being around the sick and someone I loved, it got harder to see her in the shape she was and to accept the fact that one day, the woman whose bed I would climb into in the middle of the night as a child with my blanket when my mom was alive, the person who was there the day of my tragedy, sharing similar hurt, the one who had reminded me of a time when things were normal, would tell me how much my mother loved me and who could bridge the distance between "what was" and "what is," would soon live in heaven and abandon me as well.

I began trying to mentally, physically and emotionally prepare. I couldn't bear the hurt, so I selfishly began to disconnect. While she was slowly deteriorating, I would go pick up the kids on a biweekly or weekly basis so they could get out and have fun. Aunt Mira had been my savior and I promised myself in return that I would make sure her children had all they needed to help them succeed and strive.

I failed to hug her often and tell her how much I loved her before her day came. Although I know she knew I loved her deeply and was fully aware of my level of discomfort around the sick, I just wished I could've been comfortable enough to just lay with her in my arms or me in hers and just talk. Tell her my most intimate feelings, secrets, life plans or to just hear her breathe her last breath. I wish I had had more opportunities and time between my two jobs and school to dedicate. We went outside and took walks, but as she got sicker, she walked a lot slower and needed to sit down frequently. To not know the time or day she would leave me all alone until we meet again in heaven, there was no way to fully mentally, physically and emotionally plan for that day.

I became addicted to alcohol. I found myself drinking every day to numb my pain. And there was a serious need to be in environments where everyone was carefree and careless. When I wasn't drinking, I was in a dark place, alone and zoned out. I became a functional and responsible alcoholic. I would drink and maybe party all night. After parties, I always made it home safe, napped and was up in time for work. I found and still find peace on the dance floor. It is where I zone out and the music takes me to another place in time. All of my tensions and stresses are released. I leave a club spot always feeling refreshed.

Over the years, the need for a drink and intake decreased tremendously. Now when I drink, it's primarily in social settings. But at the time, many situations in my life contributed to my actions and reactions and my need to indulge in a stimulant or depressant. Never drugs, thankfully.

My concentration in school had dwindled. So I was once again placed on academic probation. With six months "off," I threw my attention toward other extracurricular activities, which became an escape. Having free time to sit and think about what was going on in my life wasn't the plan. It in fact did more harm than good.

My tragedy haunted me while I was awake and during any free moment I had to think. The two people inside me battled. My weaker self wanted it all to end and the only way for it to end was to kill myself because there was just no hope. My stronger and more reasonable self avoided free time for thinking, by any means necessary. I sought out opportunities as necessary to keep focused, sane and balanced.

I started fashion modeling. My reasoning was I would work on my shyness by getting rid of my stage fright and getting out of my tomboy look. It was in a different borough, where no one knew my name.

I had recently gotten my first relaxer after many years of having my hair straightened every Sunday and it becoming a nappy Afro puff again after just a couple of days of sweating. I had a face full of teenage acne that stood out and shined like Rudolf's nose on a dark night. I didn't think I was quite model material, but others seemed to think differently.

My introduction to the modeling world was by doing runway shows. Modeling helped changed my perception of myself. I remember getting my first photo shoot pictures back, and I was stunned by the beautiful woman who had been captured in the photo and was staring back at me. I distinctly remember asking if it had been photo-shopped. I had never taken the time to look at myself in the mirror all that long, nor did I truly care about who I was or would become. I had no real sense of self, dignity or pride. It was almost as if my steps were being controlled by others and not by me.

My first show was the biggest and I was very happy with the outcome. I was in a group of women of all shapes and sizes. Because of my height and build, there were many options for me. I was the last to come out, dressed in the most daring outfits. I did a number of shows and modeled some upcoming styles and brands of clothing that I had not heard of. Modeling was an outlet. It was something that was fun and gave me a sense of self and freedom.

In the first scene, I closed out wearing a beaded silver dress with a sexy boy-short-style panty and bra set underneath. Another scene, I rocked this red, fitted spandex dress with cutout circles in various parts of the dress.

I don't remember everyone who came to that show, but I knew Ms. Carol was coming and that meant so much to me because her son and I had broken up; it was then that I understood that she would always be there for me. There are some people who will always have a special place in my life. We still keep in touch today. She is an amazing woman and mother. Thanksgiving with this family was one I looked forward to and would make it my last stop, if not my only stop. She is an awesome cook and knows how to set the tone for the family, which is what I've always yearned for and have grown to love. Sixteen years have passed and the love is still alive.

Ms. Carol wasn't the only person to attend my shows. My aunt was another I remember being there also. There were many who said they would come and didn't leaving me feeling disappointment. I often invited people involved in my life to come support me in my events, and when I walked out on the runway and looked around, I hoped to hear someone shout out my name.

Sometimes celebrities were in the building. Rappers 50 Cent and LL Cool J showed up during one of my shows at a hotel in Queens. I walked out and they were in the middle of a rap battle. This was during 50's early years of rapping when he had the rap about robbing everyone. It was a very interesting and entertaining performance. However, the attention was focused more on the artists than the show.

But while modeling was an outlet, it didn't solve all my problems. I was still drinking. Many times before hitting the runway, I recall taking a couple shots of the Henny, which was always available to us. I guess my intention to use modeling to overcome stage fright was defeated, as I never walked the runway without alcohol. Liquor was my savior and comforter.

****

So I remained determined to stay busy. While still out of school, I started searching for another job that would pay more and provide more of a challenge. I landed a job at Fleet Bank on Park Avenue.

The change in scenery in my work world increased my ability to approach and accept mental challenges. These challenges kept me focused and part of life.

My experience at Fleet is one that will always live with me. I experienced such personal development and an increased level of responsibility, and the lifelong friendships I developed I still maintain today just as with my previous jobs.

I first started as a teller and in a short time moved up to be the senior business teller responsible for $1.3 million. There was no protective glass between me and my customers, which allowed me to meet and get to know individuals from various companies. My personality was perfect for customer service positions and customers were quite comfortable and pleased with my service.

My supervisor, Thelma Rogers, was the best. She took me under her wing and trained me on the position, and also coached me on how to deal and cope in the world of banking, which was unfamiliar to me. She was Italian and called me her chocolate daughter and she had a great deal of respect and faith in me that I would be something great one day. She was close to retirement age, but had no plans of retiring or moving to another state to be with her daughter. She would often say, "When I die, I want my coffin to be right next to Diamond's teller station."

The rapport that I maintained, from my peers to my managers, was and has always been professional and cordial. I remembered after some time working at Fleet and not many knowing what was going on in my personal life, the branch manager called me into the office. I had just had the fistfight with my uncle and the bruises on my arm were visible. I was unaware they were showing as I always tried to wear a blazer while in the office, but at some point I had forgotten about the bruises and taken off my blazer without thinking anything of it. The branch manager had called me in to tell me what a wonderful job I was doing and that he had requested a raise effective immediately. He then said, "I don't know what's going on in your personal life but I hope this raise is enough to get you out of your situation and in to a new." I was shocked, yet grateful. Looking for a stable home was my next focus. My branch manager was yet another person who had seen my potential and wanted better for me.

I achieved many milestones during my time at Fleet. I earned a raise that made my income high enough to secure and maintain an apartment. I achieved my undergraduate degree and gave birth to my first-born. Undeniably, the friends I met then and have recently reunited with have been nothing shy of the best.

Martha the security guard was my favorite. She was hood fabulous and kept me laughing. Although our positions, duties and responsibilities were serious, she cracked jokes all day. (After leaving Fleet, I remember like it was yesterday, the day she called me and told me that she was ill and might not live too much longer. My heart sunk and I quickly made it a point to keep in touch and make plans to see her more often.)

Diana was the first person I met at Fleet. She was older and was another who helped me get through some trying days. She also found a friend in me and began to open up and share her personal life and I reciprocated once I felt as comfortable. In our down times, we would talk about any and everything that was on our minds and did our best to help each other through our struggles. We were the longest-serving tellers there and had seen many come and go. She moved on to be a customer service representative and me a business teller.

I then met Clarissa who introduced me to the world of Brooklyn. She had invited me to her son's christening. I couldn't attend due to my own obligations, but it was then that I realized that our friendship had begun. I found myself hanging out with her after work and got to know her family. I later became the godmother of her daughter Chloe and she the godmother to my daughter.

Then there were Nicole and Marissa. Each has been a part of many meaningful events in my life. We encourage each other through our daily struggles and still keep in touch and hang out when we can. Nicole was a little younger than me and lived out in Staten Island, which was a troop for both of us, but if there was an event she was having, I made my way from the Bronx to the boat. She also made it a point to come to the Bronx to support any of my functions.

Both Marissa and Nicole had a wonderful relationship with their mothers. Each respected their mothers and their mothers always had their back. Both mothers were so calm and caring. They became people I gravitated toward when spending time with Marissa and Nicole. I always felt a part of the family. The words of wisdom from both mothers that I would leave with were food for thought, food that never went bad and would always be useful regarding the many things I faced. Our friendships developed into something of a sister, sister relationship.

It feels good to go through the ups and downs of life with someone, whether it's your friends or your family. When you have made it to the top of the mountain, there is much you will not see when you look down because everything seems so distant. Such is life. The memory of the issues and processes fades, relationships with the people who walk the walk with you grow and the experience strengthens you.

There are many of my Fleet customers still in my life today also. One guy named Cameron adored me and the feelings were mutual, though I didn't know his feelings at the time. But I know much better today. We worked in the same building and he would frequently show his face in the bank. I would receive flower arrangements just because and very thoughtful birthday gifts. He asked to take me out on a date and it was refreshing with all that I had going on. He was my escape. The perfect gentleman with children. We went to the movies and the Promenade in Brooklyn. We walked and talked and gazed out at the East River, the Brooklyn Bridge and all the lights. At our age, it was the most romantic experience I had had. The feeling was surreal. After our date, he made sure I got to my door safely. Because of the mental space I was in, I didn't feel deserving of this man and knew nothing of commitment, especially a man who seemed to be the full package. I was so lost in the world and wasn't fit to be a role model to anyone. I was in a place and space in my life that wasn't healthy for anyone. Not even myself. We remained friends and kept in touch throughout the years.

As a business teller, I primarily took care of company accounts and change orders. The world is so small because although most of us have all moved on in life, after 13 years, I still bump into them either through a mutual friend, enjoying nightlife or summer events.

Ricky was one of them. He worked at a nearby Au Bon Pain and would come in with his team to make deposits for his company. They would frequently bring us goodies, which was something we looked forward to. When I became pregnant, the meals and treats were daily. Reconnecting with him after all these years brought me back to a time when I was not as mentally and emotionally strong. Yet the people in my world kept me on an even keel.

Having someone who cares about you and what goes on in your life without motive is rare. So I hold tight to the ones I have found who care and have consistently shown the same. We all face things in life and at different times. There is a point in our lives when we all need something or someone to help get us to that next phase of life. If your help is genuine, the reward for giving comes with no expectations.

And it was at Fleet that I got the news that Aunt Mira had passed away. In hindsight, it probably was for the best that when I got the news I was around people who had become like family to me. I remember the day like it was yesterday.

I was at work when I received a beep on my pager, with a message telling me to call Uncle Steve, my aunt Mira's common-law husband. It was strange because my uncle never called me. It didn't dawn on me that something must be wrong. So I waited until I counted everyone's cash box out for the day. When I finally called to speak to Uncle Steve, I was told that Aunt Mira had already died. Her youngest son, Isaiah, came home from school and walked in the room to kiss his mom and let her know that he was home. When she did not move, he got scared and called the ambulance and his dad.

I was so devastated. I went numb and do not remember my reactions directly following the news. I blacked out.

It was only the weekend before that she had asked me to take her to the carnival that was opening that year near the Bronx Zoo. But had started working a second job at Benetton Sisley on Fifth Avenue and had just started taking college classes again. There was so much going on that when I wasn't busy, I was sleeping. She kept calling me to confirm our outing but each time I was busy with the above. In doing so, I never got to speak with her again. I was so deeply torn. If only I could've granted what I didn't know would be her last wish.

From this and other deaths before, I have made a promise to myself to make every last visit and conversation count. Make good on all of my promises. Resolve all issues before the close of the night. Give myself just 24 to 48 hours to be in my feelings of anger. I find myself frequently sending out email or text blasts just reaching out to tell the people in my circle that I love them and to let them know they have been on my mind.

Deaths leave a lot of "what ifs," and "shoulda, coulda, wouldas." Regrets have helped me do better with the people I have left in my life. The negative side to this for me is that it consumes me and I am constantly mentally preparing for deaths to minimize the hurt I could potentially feel. Instead of just freely living and being the good person that I am, I think about death, which is most familiar and a part of life for me and restricts my thinking and living.

****

I was completely out of it after getting the news about Aunt Mira, and my supervisor called a guy I had started dating recently to come pick me up and escort me home. The guy's name was Cornell. He was so sweet. He had the cutest dimples, a baldhead and was on the stocky side. Such a charmer and very sensitive. When I cried he felt compelled to cry. We had met through Nicole who was dating his twin brother. He worked a block away from my job so we spent a lot of time after work. He lived in Queens and I lived in the Bronx, which made it difficult to spend time on the weekends. But Sundays was football day with his friends, so I would join in and try to understand the sport just to spend time with him.

Cornell rushed over to my job from work that day and took the train with me to the Bronx to view my aunt's body before they prepared to take her to the morgue. Reality had not set in. She was my best friend, my heart and soul. On the train ride up, I started to reflect on the many memories as I lay in his arms and cried. He was just the kind of man I needed at this time and hour in my life.

I was a zombie as I walked into her building in Parkchester. As I got to her floor, there was a smell that would become stamped in my memory bank. Whenever I went to visit after she had long gone, the scent would still be there. I was able to see her in her bed before they covered her up. Although I knew how sick she had become, how much medication she consumed daily, the pain and frustration she endured for her family having to do for her what she would have normally done when she was well. Finally, the fact that she had no energy to be an active part of her boys' life still didn't help with my understanding of why she had to go. Why was the pain deeper than any I had ever remembered?

Every morning like clockwork, she would call me at 6:30 and say, "Rise and shine, sunshine." Or sing, "Good morning to you, good morning to you, we're all in our places with sunshiny faces and this is the way to start a new day." This is the morning anthem I now sing to my baby girl to get her day started.

We had found out about a month before my aunt took her last breath that Uncle Bob, Elijah's father, had died. It was so sad because we were all close growing up. He embraced and cared for us like his own. When we left the South he still kept in touch.

My grandma was in shambles. She had now lost a second daughter. We managed to get things together for the funeral considering the high level of emotional distress. The one stressor for most minority families after death strikes is not having insurance or written wills. We didn't have much money to bury her, so we all agreed to have her cremated. It was rough. I felt so empty, lost and without direction. My brother had been released from jail and made it back to New York in time to make the funeral. My Uncle Marvin was still away in a mental institution. I was unable to locate him, so he was unable to see her for the last time.

Life for me will never be the same. Despite a greater understanding today, it is not the same as having her here in the flesh, but she is always with me in spirit, and I am never alone. My aunt and mother pay me visits in my dreams frequently with lots of laughs, hugs and kisses shared. After a visit, I usually wake up feeling refreshed and refueled to continue life here on earth.

****

The semester had begun pretty well, but the ending was rough. I couldn't get it together and couldn't focus. I fell into a deep depression. Once again, I turned to alcohol to numb my pain. I had shut down and didn't want to be bothered. I could not bear to see Elijah and Isaiah because I couldn't be strong for them. It hurt too much. I wasn't sure where to turn or who to talk to so, I agreed to seek professional help. First, I needed my school to know what was going on because I had just gotten off academic probation with the drama in my household. I was scheduled almost immediately to speak to a counselor. Talking to him didn't help me at all. He advised me to try to focus on my midterms and get through the semester. I also had to prepare for a proficiency exam, one I had failed the first time because I hadn't opened the book to study and prep beforehand. My issues were bigger than me.

I went to my regular physician because I was skipping my monthly cycles. It skipped almost three months at a time, and when it did come, I bled heavier than usual. I was told it was stress that was causing my hormones to go out of whack. I also expressed the things I was going through and was referred over to the mental health department. I was prescribed Prozac for depression. But my need for alcohol was at a high and was my addiction. I was in control while intoxicated, and although I didn't know my limits, I was very familiar with the effects. I had no desire to get addicted to any drugs and learn its affects. So I decided against it.

I would often sit at my desk at Fleet and daydream, but had no clear thoughts. My co-worker Clarissa was worried and reported me to the supervisor when she saw me in a daze, playing with my letter opener. I was instructed to get help through the Human Resource hotline. Again, I found it not to be effective.

I was always able to speak about my issues and recognize my problems. I was just too weak and couldn't figure out a way to solve them. I instead found coping methods to take me away from my current state of thinking. What I did have a problem with was talking to people who couldn't relate, but gave me advice based on what they had studied. This is why my sessions were never successful. My counselors and therapists were just trained to listen and give me ideas about how to cope with my issues. That was the answer all along, but back then I was too far-gone to understand it. I wanted things to be fixed and all to be normal again and for someone to fully relate and truly understand my sorrow.

I was always hesitant to go to church because the pastor was a representative of my enemy: God! Eventually, I put those feelings aside and another avenue opened was attending church; the lessons and sermons that the pastor gave were powerful and personal. I always felt he understood me. He knew my pain and sorrow.

But trying to be the best that I could be under the circumstances, continued to get more and more difficult as reality set in. I was all alone in this huge world. My screams were unheard and my tears ducts were dry. I was weak and lifeless with no strength to defend myself if I was attacked.

I began to think of the things I had done that were sinful. Everyone commits sin whether big or small. I was finding it hard to get close to people due to my feeling of not wanting God to take them away from me once I got attached and loved them. My focus was all over the place and life was just unbearable for me.

I had thoughts of suicide often. I imagined throwing myself in front of a moving train.
For some reason, every train seemed to move slower into the station than normal. I thought of just walking onto a busy highway in front of high-speed moving cars. In both instances, the possibility of instant death was not guaranteed. In fact, doing so may have also caused harm to someone else, which was definitely not part of my plan. Someone swerving their car trying to prevent hitting me could cause a six-car pileup, or something, and many other deaths. I was not interested in a slow death either, with the possibility of more pain, but one that would be quick and painless. I was too much of a coward to follow through.

Something in my mind was telling me that there was a reason I survived. That split second of how Mommy was able to save me is something that kept me searching for my purpose.

But the amount of pain suffered at that moment deepened. It consumed me and it was almost as if that was all I knew. Pain became a part of me. A hardened shell. I wasn't easily moved by any of the achievements I had made because it didn't matter. It was merely something to do to keep my mind preoccupied from the negative thinking.

In those moments that life didn't matter when I was younger, I found myself engaging in activities that discredited my character. I started dancing on tabletops for fun. All it took was a few shots of Hennessy to get me started. Doing whatever came to mind without thought. The problem with dancing on table tops, which led to a quick end to that experience, was not being comfortable being touched or with having to take off pieces of my clothes to expose my body parts. If I couldn't perform with a nice two-piece, it wasn't happening. I got by with that twice. I was guarded and my wishes were granted. On the third attempt, touching and getting naked was mandated and that was the day I walked away.

It was the most dangerous, yet free, era in my life. Being taken advantage of by men I thought had my best interest at heart. All because I made them look good. I was the trophy on their arm, as a couple of them put it. The lies that came with it of me being underage and one being in his upper 20s and the other well into his 30s.

I remember a sponsor of my modeling club, Kahiem, approached me after I had seen him for many months at my shows and photo shoots, and asked me to marry him. Not go on a date with him with the hopes that I would be his girlfriend, but straight to marriage.

He was tall, dark-skinned with a nice, low-cut Caesar, a nice grade of hair and well dressed. He drove a Range Rover and wore many pieces of diamond jewelry. He was very attractive, though far from my type because he was too flashy and known to too many. He appeared to be a ladies' man.

A few times, he would drive a few of the models to the train station. Never uttered anything more than "hello and thank you." But while at my lingerie and swimwear photo shoot, he felt it was appropriate to pop the question. Considering the position I was in, my being alone with just him and his dear friend and client, who was also my manager and photographer, I didn't know what either was capable of and I needed to get out of that space safely. I respectfully declined and explained to him that we didn't know each other that way.

I was all of 20 years old. I was going through many things in my family and was in between households, but I wasn't in need of a meal or rescue ticket. I didn't need saving. He was in his late 20s, early 30s. My manager chimed in to try to convince me that he was a big deal. He was the reason the studio existed. This didn't sway my decision. He then threatened to keep the photos that I had just taken and take me out of the big shows that were coming up. Kahiem then said, "Are you aware of what would happen if your photos started floating around the Web and in the streets?" With no care in the world I told him that with as much porn as there was in the world, it wouldn't be the first time anyone saw a half-naked woman.

I grabbed my things and left. My manager stuck to his word. I wasn't called for any shows after that. My modeling days with him ended. Years later, Kahiem would be wanted on rape, murder and child molestation charges. My manager would go on to wed a 19-year-old while in his 50s. I was happy to have escaped the situation unharmed. These men preyed on young women.

It was at that moment that I became fully aware of how some men operate. Then, some months later, I met a guy named Ben. He was about nine years older than me and he explained how older men view younger women. He was cool. We hung out often and became really good friends. After a year, he proposed. But despite what we had, I wasn't ready to be in something that serious when I wasn't where I felt I wanted to be mentally, physically and emotionally. To love someone deeply out of fear they would be taken away from me wasn't what I was ready for. His being there as my shoulder and to escape was what I needed and cherished but looking that far into the future was impossible for me. I declined. "What's the rush?" I asked. He replied that other than the fact that he cared for and loved me, I was young and he didn't want me to grow older and bitter like most women out here. "Older men like younger women so they can mold them," is what he said. More of a reason for my decision to decline, even though there were feelings there. I saw him about six years later and talk of marriage was still the topic.

In all my efforts to keep preoccupied with various activities to mask the pain I felt, I found that disappointment and pain still exist. I was lost and needed to have a better understanding of my purpose. Who I am out of the millions of people here on earth? Why have I been chosen to endure the pain I have thus far? To have suffered and been forced to walk these streets alone. The need is there to have someone be there for me, fear taps at my heart and has impaired my mind to believe that this may never be possible.

Just when all was beginning to heal, I received a phone call at midnight one night. It was an officer who had worked at my high school. He had frequently called when my brother was caught doing wrong to let me know what was going on. This night's call was of a different nature. He asked if I could view a body that was believed to be my aunt Deidre's.

Nervously, I agreed. I couldn't go by myself. I phoned and stopped by the house of the guy I was dating at the time to see if he would come with me. But when I got no answer, I went to my grandmother's to let her know and to take her with me. She lost it, but was strong enough to accompany me.

We arrived at the morgue and it was Aunt Deidre. She had been stabbed multiple times, blood left in trails throughout the apartment she was murdered in. Police believed drugs were involved, but that was never confirmed.

It was painful calling Aunt Deidre's daughter, Nikkia, who was still living down South with her grandparents, to let her know. Since I had taken her there to live with her grandparents, Nikkia had never seen her mother again. My aunt Deidre had made plans to go spend time with her, but never made it. I felt a great sense of guilt for the pain Nikkia felt. She had missed her mom despite calling to speak to her, as her mother was far-gone and doing her own thing. I couldn't explain to a child that her mother was not fit to be a productive part of or play an active role in her life due to her drug consumption and lifestyle. I had hoped my aunt would turn her life around for her daughter and they would reunite and be that much better. She had been running the streets for years. Aunt Deidre had taken my mother's death really hard. Losing her only remaining sister, Aunt Mira, who was her best friend, was just too much for her to handle. She had lost everything, including her daughter, and had become reckless with her life and others around her.

Deidre's father didn't take her death well at all. He managed to bring Nikkia, along with other relatives, to the funeral but was unable to stay for the burial. Without that closure, Nikkia suffers a lot today. It is just something about seeing a casket lowered into the ground. Death becomes real. She missed that, and in addition has many other unanswered questions about why her mother couldn't get it together to be what she wanted and needed her to be. Over the years, I have been Nikkia's everything. Whatever she needs, I have been there. I send for her on holidays to spend time with us to let her know that she is never alone.

It is all so easy to encourage, motivate and inspire another going through similar experiences and pain. However, as a person like myself who is beginning to heal many years later, know that it is much easier said than done, as most things in life.

After the passing of my aunt Deidre, a customer who resembled my mother came into the Fleet Bank where I worked. She even had the same name as my mom. It was as if she had been sent from heaven to give me the strength needed to continue going forward. She was a model and would come in every so often to cash her check. She was stunning. Everyone who wasn't aware that I didn't have a mother would ask if she was. We became friends.

When I became pregnant, and she came into the bank to give me a winter-white Pooh Bear. It was such a beautiful gesture. She even went so far as to attend the baby shower. We lost touch, reconnected, and then lost touch again.

Some people are not meant to be in your life forever. Seasonal people have a purpose and should be taken as just that.

A LIFE WITH NEW MEANING—BLESSED

The birth of my daughter, Star, was like a light at the end of the darkest tunnel. The day she was born changed my whole life forever. The joy of my new bundle freed me from all sadness and filled a very huge void. It is amazing how something or someone so small could make that much of a difference in one's life. The many thoughts of uncertainty I had before she arrived were no longer a factor.

After finding out I was pregnant, I had spent many days trying to imagine what life would be like with a child. Who would baby-sit while I went to work and school? Considering how uncomfortable I was with hospitals and seeing blood, how would I manage if there were a situation in which my child got hurt and needed me? Would I have enough patience to the best mother I could be? They say sleep is the cousin of death. Due to my level of depression, sleep was my comforter. Would I hear my child when she cries in the middle of the night and have the energy to be an active part of her life? Finally, would I be able to break this generational cycle of mine and be an active listener and supporter in her life?

A couple of years before pregnancy, I had gone in for a physical exam and expressed feelings of pain in the areas of my stomach where I had been cut. After a sonogram, I was told there seemed to be some scarring and it may not be fully healed. I also was told it might be a difficult to get pregnant because of where I was wounded. Oddly enough, that had seemed false because my wounds aren't near my reproductive organs. I had never tried to get pregnant to test the waters, so I just went on with life with the thought of no possibility.

Shortly before finding out I was pregnant, I had gone out to the Mars 2112 nightclub. Mars is one of my favorite venues. After about two hours there, I felt uncomfortable and nauseous. I left. I had no desire to drink or dance. I was very nauseous, but couldn't vomit.

For the next couple of months, I continued to get my period. At this time, I was seeing a man named Anthony, and one day I woke up at his house to find him watching me. He said, "You are pregnant." I felt nauseous, but I quickly frowned on the idea. I was in serious denial. He and I had our regular weekend brunch date during which I ordered tea, which was unusual. I tried everything to get rid of the nausea and to get my taste buds back.

I finally took a home pregnancy test because my body was going through changes, and the test came back positive. I then went to the doctor, and after both a urine and blood test, my pregnancy was confirmed. I was shocked and my feelings were bittersweet. The thought of the unknown is always frightening. The difference with the process of pregnancy is that you have nine months to get familiar with the idea.

I had started dating my daughter's father in the midst of my being between houses, sometime after the death of my aunt Mira but before my aunt Deidre died. He was very attentive, something I needed in those moments. I had met him through a friend. However, we had attended the same high school as well, which made him familiar. He lived a block away from my grandmother, but with the many activities I had going on, I had never seen him in the area. We exchanged numbers and he had made himself available to drive me where I needed to go whenever I needed. I didn't immediately take advantage of the opportunity, but after seeing him more frequently, it became easier to take him up on the offer. He started driving me out to my modeling rehearsals and faithfully picking me up from school at night. He was there to help with my apartment search and with the move-in. He became a part of my daily life. He had a son and seemed to balance his time well. When we weren't at work or I at school, we would spend time watching movies or on dinner dates over the weekend, leaving very little time for ourselves. He never officially asked me to be the woman in his life; he just simply said it was understood. Time went by and he was being invited to friends' and family events and I was introduced to his family. The friendship and relationship was an easy flow.

After some time, he began to become distant and seemed to be hiding something. I didn't notice it immediately because of my day-to-day activities and his consistency. It became more obvious that night I needed him to come with me to view my aunt Deidre's body when I received that midnight phone call and couldn't find him despite calling him and going by his house to ring his bell. The lies started, with one lie leading to many more over time. We were on the brink of going our separate ways. I was finally on a better path in school. I had taken my first vacation out of the country to Mexico. I was breaking free and treading different waters. When I came back to New York from Mexico, I was certain that this wasn't the man for me. Mainly due to his distance and all that I felt he was hiding. There was a serious disconnection. He was a man of very few words but was very big on action. However, I needed to hear how he felt and what was going on in his head. I knew he cared for me. But I was unsure if we were going in the same direction. Despite knowing better, I went back and forth because I didn't truly understand my worth and what I deserved. There was a sense of familiarity and comfort in being with him. As most of my loved ones had loved me but continuously hurt me, this was a normal feeling. We sat and made an attempt to talk before we both agreed to go our separate ways, which led to us having one more intimate moment for the road. We continued seeing each other.

Finding out I was pregnant was yet another challenge along the road of trials and tribulations I had experienced. You never truly learn a person until you have various experiences with them. Even then, many responses to situations can change depending on the moment.

He expressed to me that he wasn't ready for any more children and needed time away to think. We had never spoken of having kids but we were engaging in activities that would produce kids. Selfishly, I had made the decision to have my baby whether she had a father to be a part of her life or not.

What was supposed to be a joyous and memorable moment, turned out to be the worst emotional roller coaster one could imagine. From attending doctor appointments alone to finding out that I wasn't the only woman in his life expecting a baby, it was devastating. My depression was at a high. My emotions played a big role in how sick I was. I was anticipating the nausea going away after the first trimester, but I went the full duration of throwing up day in and day out. I even threw up the day I was giving birth. After work, I would make it home and after a quick shower, would go straight to bed. I was given a doctor's note requesting to take one day off per week. With the years I had put in at Fleet, I was granted the time needed.

My pregnancy was a shock to me and it took me a while to share it with many. I was almost five months along before I shared the news with Grandmother Meena and Aunt Mira's husband, Uncle Steve. When I called my grandmother, I told her I needed to see her so that I could share something with her. She responded, "What, are you pregnant?" I wasn't expecting that response, but like a child, I said, "Yes, Grandma." She went on to say that I was grown, had a job and lived on my own so she didn't see a reason why I wouldn't have my baby. I was relieved and felt more comfortable in my decision. Sometimes all you need is one supporter to fulfill a dream.

It was exciting to hear my baby's heart beating but it became real when I felt her first kick one evening while I was in class. It felt as if there was a fish swimming inside me. As she grew and her space got smaller her movements slowed and had my stomach on a tilt at times when her kicking was harder. It was such a beautiful experience.

Her father slowly started coming around to bring foods that I craved. Took me food shopping and consistently started picking me up from school again whether we spoke or not. One night he said he had something to tell me and we detoured and took a ride. I was nervous because when he had to share something with me, it would always be something that threw me for a loop. However, I was prepared for whatever he had to say. He then took that time to share that he had purposely gotten me pregnant so he would be able to see me for the rest of his life. So many emotions came over me at that very moment but couldn't respond. I asked, "Why did you put me through everything that I had suffered so far?" He answered,

"Because doing it purposely would have been made obvious." It hurt so bad that this was a game to him.

I realized at that moment that I had not had much control in my life and the things that took place in my world. Everyone and everything had been situations that forced me to be involved and make decisions. But I have no regrets as on the flipside, it helped to be a part of life creating lasting memories.

After his revelation, we pulled up to a Sears where he bought me a video camera for a Christmas gift. This was to be used to capture memorable moments for my new bundle. Over the years we were together, I received the best gifts ever. Much of what I felt derived out of the guilt he felt from his actions. I was grateful nonetheless.

I was in constant prayer. I prayed for clarity about my situation. There were so many unanswered questions. Through signs I receive God's messages. The day had finally come when all was revealed. Something concrete. I was in my sixth month and my energy level was at a low, my sickness had increased and the baby was growing rapidly. We were having a potluck at my job and I was asked to bring small items. It was the day before the potluck, a Sunday, and I had been lying around all day. I had made two attempts to head to the supermarket to get what I needed for the following day. I was entering the forgetful stage of pregnancy and it was annoying. I finally made my way to the supermarket and got a block away before realizing that I had left the shopping cart. I had to go back home. Ended up sitting down for an hour or so.

At that point, I had no choice but to go, and fast, because the store would be closing soon. When I finally got there, I saw Anthony's car. I pulled out my phone to call him but realized this may be my sign from God. I walk into the supermarket and see him with his kid's mother. I had found out sometime after we started dating that he had another child, a little girl. I realized as a man and father, he should be in the supermarket helping his child's mother with their kid's groceries. I would want the same for me and mine. I was more curious about how he would react when he saw me. I made my rounds to get what I needed and when I made it back to the front of the store, I was face to face with him. He froze and just stared at me. I said, "Hi." And he didn't respond. I then said, "So you do not know me now?" He just stared at me. I was pissed. I pushed past him and continued my shopping. When I left the store, he was in his car and just watched me walk away. At that point, I knew what it was. There was no need to think there was hope in an "us." I felt betrayed. Or should I have? Should she feel betrayed? From the looks of it, they were together in a relationship and I was the side chick. I could not bear to think that that was the category I was in. I was so disgusted, numb and there were no tears present to release.

God moves and works in mysterious ways. There always seem to be a distraction to take me away from moments that could've sent me to the crazy home.

When I got back home and settled, I received a phone call from someone claiming to be my sister. I vaguely remembered her when she came to the hospital with my father the day he stole from me. She had gotten my number from my aunt and needed to talk to someone. She nervously shared with me that she was pregnant and had been hiding it and didn't know what to do and who to talk to. I felt that much better to know that I could be something more to someone than I felt I was to myself at times. The issues I had were nothing compared to my little sister who was 17 at the time and in her last year of high school. We talked for awhile and she promised that she would stay focused and finish school and I told her that I would be down to visit once I had given birth and my baby had had her shots at 2 months old. Her baby was due to be born a month before mine.

There is always someone experiencing more difficulties than you. It didn't take away from what I had going on or how I was feeling, however, I was rescued from dealing with my issues at hand. I tend to do better dealing with issues when seconds, hours and days have passed and I could think more rationally.

I struggled emotionally and physically through the rest of my pregnancy. My sciatic nerve started bothering me and made it more difficult to walk. As the baby grew, pressure on the nerve grew. In my last trimester, I learned I was borderline diabetic. It was the most difficult last days. The only meal I could keep down was peanut butter and jelly sandwiches. I had to change the bread I normally used to whole wheat minus the jelly to satisfy that craving. I was advised to use Equal, Sweet and Low or Splenda artificial sugars, all of which I prefer today. At the beginning of my last month, I was tapped out and physically unable to make that trip to work. I took the time needed to rest and patiently wait for my blessing to arrive.

Such as with most experiences, as you get closer to your goal, things get more challenging to test your strength.

I later found out that the women I had seen in the supermarket with my soon-to-be daughter's father had a more serious situation and they were expecting another child of their own. I was livid. Hulk Hogan mad. This was not how I imagined my first pregnancy experience would be.

I realized you have to expect the unexpected when you are dealing with people. The disappointment and internal hurt was at a high and it seemed no matter how hard I tried, I couldn't escape the hurt. After some time passed and reality set in, I took it with a grain of salt and began to come up with a plan. My little one and I against the world was how this would be. I managed to finish out my last classes, making it 12 more to complete before graduation at that time, before giving birth.

I had two beautiful big baby showers. My job had given me one and my family and friends had given and attended the other. I got everything that I needed and more. In fact, I was blessed with three strollers, four high chairs and swings and three bouncers along with other much needed items. I was more than appreciative. That was the start of what marked the many days of blessings ahead. I have been blessed beyond belief with everything needed to raise my little one. Many doors of opportunity became visible answering all of the many questions and concerns I had during pregnancy.

The week before I was due to have my baby girl, I went in to see my doctor and to my surprise, she said I would have my baby before the weekend. I left the doctor's office and walked about 20 or more blocks that day while talking to a good friend Malcolm on the phone. It was always refreshing to have good people around to fill in the gaps or connect bridges so I can get by and keep sane.

That evening I went to the hospital because I was in a tremendous amount of pain from contractions and was sent home because I wasn't dilated. I went home and throughout the night the contractions got greater and closer in minutes. I couldn't sleep, sit or lay down. I paced the floor all night until about 5:30 a.m. Anthony took me back to the hospital, where I was admitted immediately. The nurses had me walk around a bit to help with the labor. Around 10:30 a.m., my pain was unbearable and I was given the epidural. The feeling was amazing. After eight hours, the medicine wore off and the pains started again. It was now time to push. With the medication in my system, I couldn't feel any contractions to prompt me to push. My Grandma Meena, cousin Janet, friend Asia and Anthony were all by my side. I was given three hours to push or a cesarean would be the end result. Within two hours and forty-four minutes, I was able to push her out. In the last hour, most things tend to unfold. It was all captured on video.

Years later, Star saw the video of her birth and was mesmerized. She asked me if it hurt, then expressed how sorry she was if she had hurt me.

But now, my angel had arrived and I was so delirious, she was taken from me the first night but brought to me around 6a.m. the following morning. The doctors came in to apply pressure to my stomach, pressing all the way down to my abs. I felt so disgusting. I wanted to take a bath and move around. My fear of hospitals and flashbacks of my first hospital stay were haunting me. But I had my taste buds back. That was a happy thing, and I had a huge craving for a McDonald's cheeseburger.

I made an attempt to go to the bathroom, only to have a trail of blood following my steps. I was so embarrassed. I was wearing the hospital pads, but it was just too much blood. Something more to toy with my mind, and bring back bad memories. I quickly got the attention of one of the hospital janitors for a mop, and it happened to be someone I had worked with at Pergament. I was embarrassed but he put me at ease. He would stop in to check on me throughout my time in the hospital. Though it was nice to have a familiar face around, I was so ready to go home after Day 2. The nurses gave me my discharge information for that very evening, but said if I stayed until the following morning, they would have gifts for me. Day 3, I was released and I must admit, as a new mother, I was very scared to go home and take care of a little person who couldn't take care of herself. I needed company and it was very helpful having my grandmother's sister, Aunt Marie, and friends come over. I was able to run out to get girdles to assist with reducing my tummy, along with getting some air. The breastfeeding went very well.

There is no handbook on the do's and don'ts of parenting, but my goal was to provide and expose my daughter to much of what I had yearned for growing up. She was my new little experiment, my investment. My own live doll baby. Where I lived was so serene. There were many houses and trees, similar to my childhood setting. We would take long strolls around the block to get some air while I hummed songs to her.

Unfortunately, it wasn't long before drama intruded once again. After a couple of months, my daughter's father and I were at that same supermarket shopping, when out of nowhere, a woman ran up on me and snuffed me; no words said. Seconds later, we were having an all-out fistfight in front of the supermarket. I had no idea who the woman was, having totally forgotten that I had seen her with my daughter's father months prior when I had bumped into them. When we were separated, she began shouting everything that I was not. Or was I? Being unaware of the nature of their relationship, I was totally offended. What made matters worse was that she lived right around the corner which meant that from that day forth there would be problems in my neighborhood and possibly at my door.
I never seeked out trouble or intentionally and knowingly went into situations that could cause harm, however it always found me.

The many signs that I couldn't or chose not to see, compiled with everything else around me falling apart, was beginning to take a toll on me. Such is life. When it rains it pours.

I had experienced many challenges in my apartment with no heat and hot water. There were many days I had to stay at Anthony's house because the boiler would be broken and my landlord didn't have the funds to pay to get it fixed in an adequate amount of time. And when she did, it was never done properly. It was definitely time to move and so I began to put a plan in action.
The final straw was a flood that damaged my baby's furniture and some of her clothing. I was on a mission to move, but needed to get away and refuel with some family love first.

There is a saying that when a baby is coming into the world, someone leaves the world.

My grandma Flore had insisted on my coming down South to visit. Due to my physical state while pregnant, my physician restricted travel. She insisted on seeing me. She kept saying she didn't think she'd make it to see her new great-granddaughter. By this time she had become blind. So the moment I had my new bundle and gotten her two months' shots, the very next day we were headed South. I took Grandma Meena with me on this trip. We had some much-needed family fun. My aunt Gail worked at a high-end hotel so we were able to get a discount on our stay.

My aunt had a nice-size house. However, she had five children ranging in age from 3 to 13. It was always exciting to watch how they interacted around each other. The bickering, the fighting simply meant they loved each other that much. When it was time to have a party, it would be fun for all. Family and friends from all over attended. There was music, card games, food on the grill and everyone mingling. Toward the end of the night, my aunt had the bug repellants and candles handy for everyone. I had a bouncer with a zip net for my little one. She was well protected from the bugs and very comfortable.

I reconnected with my sister and met my nephew. She had fulfilled her promise, so we attended her graduation while there as well. Memorable moments for sure went down in the books.

Back in New York, after a very short time of looking for a place, I found one very close to my grandma Meena. I instantly fell in love with it. Huge spacious living room with hardwood floors, tall windows and the best of all was the view. I felt as if I was on top of the world. The one thing I did not take in consideration was the many flights I had to walk up to get to the penthouse. It was a six-floor walkup with no elevator.

I once read somewhere:
There is no elevator to success. You have to take the stairs.
- Unknown

This has held true in so many instances in my life. My struggles have all led to a more meaningful outcome with great reward. Of course while I experienced the strain and struggles, I wished for an easier path because I did not know how different the outcome would be. After the sweat and tears, I feel like a warrior ready for anything else I am to face. There are some things in life that come easy. However, the level of appreciation is weighed differently.

God works in mysterious ways and timing is everything because I was looking for an apartment for a while and turned down many. I found this apartment and moved in two days before I was due to return to work after maternity leave. My neighbors were awesome and offered to help move me in and would frequently check on us. Throughout my years there, they would knock to check on us and we would reciprocate the gesture.

I was settling in my new friendly environment and had to prepare myself to go back to work. I had been off five months and it was indeed time to get back into the swing. My first month back to normalcy was difficult because I was still breastfeeding and school had resumed. My breasts would swell and become hard as rocks with pain when it was feeding time. I would rush home and breastfeed her quickly for relief. Then rush right out to school.

Although I pumped and had milk at home, this pain gave me an excuse to see her because I really missed her once I returned to work. As time went on, it was in my routine to go home before class. One day I went home and she simply shook her head "no" to the breast.

With the levels of depressions I dealt with throughout pregnancy, I was determined to bounce back by getting back into my groove of life. I never imagined that I would have a child under the circumstances that I faced. I remember in my early teenage years of having life all mapped out. In one thought, I was going to be married with a big house with a white picket fence and five children. The level of comfort I imagined with having a loving man and my own house with a bunch of a children to fill my voids of pain.
In reality, my thoughts were a fog. Dark and gloomy.

My new bundle gave me hope and that was my new focus. I had been told I was selfish to bring her into the world without being married or knowing if her father would play the huge role he is playing in her life today. The truth of the matter is I played a role in the act of creating her and the gift that was given was one that deserved to live and shine in my gloomy world. Everyone waits for the perfect situation or when she or he is financially stable or with a husband or wife. They fail to realize that there may be a better time and situation but no time is ever perfect.

Over the years, I have met many who have a husband with money and they are free to stay home and raise their child, but they never see the husband because he is working hard to take care of everything. Then there are the two-parent households where their professions monopolize most of their time and the child barely gets the attention needed other than from a sitter. I am grateful for the balance. I am able participate in her school life, go over homework with her and tuck her in every night (if I am not on a business or leisure trip).

Shortly after my return from the South and getting settled in my new apartment, I received a phone call from Grandma Flore thanking me for making all the efforts I made to see her and telling me that she loved me. Her leg had just been amputated. She felt it was time to let go and made it a point to share this as well. She died soon after. Torn and with many emotions, I couldn't pull myself together enough to make it to the funeral. It would be five years before I would find my way back down South to introduce my daughter to the family. It was nice to see and hangout with everyone, but there was clearly something missing. Grandmothers keep families together.

MANAGING

My grandmother Meena and Star's father became my sitters once I went back to work. All started out well. I was very impressed with my grandmother's behavior after having Star. I truly felt that she had finally come around to being a better grandmother to my daughter than she had been to me. I would come home and baby girl would be bathed and sleeping. The house was in good shape and dinner made. It was very helpful and convenient.

I had just gotten an offer to work at a branch closer to home with part-time hours. I would work from 10a.m. to 3p.m. I took advantage of the opportunity to take 8a.m. and 4 p.m. classes. This worked out very well, as I was able to be home with my baby sooner. But after a short time, things began to fall apart. The branch was short staffed and very busy. So on many occasions, I worked as a teller and customer service representative. There were times when my school obligations weren't met because of this. My grandmother would leave after baby-sitting and have drink fest parties at home and started showing up to my house late and hung over. One day, she came straight from central booking with a black eye to baby-sit and I was forced to call out.

One of my neighbors had introduced me to her sitter, and she agreed to watch Star three days a week with her father watching her the other two days. The first couple of weeks went well with the new sitter. The only problem for me was that she only spoke Spanish. Then a month went by, and when I picked Star up, I noticed a red mark that looked like a hickey on her forehead. I was furious and just knew I was going to lose it. The baby-sitter couldn't tell me what happen other than that she think she may have hit her head in her play yard. The words "I think" had me ready to strangle her. I envisioned myself in an orange jump suit and slippers behind bars. I just took my baby and all her things never did business with her again.

I felt like my walls were caving in on me from being overwhelmed. If I had my way, I would just take a step back and stay home with my baby until she was old enough to talk to me.

I fell into a deep depression and began to dread going to work. The bank was preparing for a merger and new rules were being implemented. When I am juggling multiple things, routine works much better for me. When the day came that my position ended, I knew God had not only heard my prayer, but also felt and understood my struggles.

I was out of work for a year and a month. But the moments shared day in and day out with my little one were so refreshing. It was a joy to wake up in the morning, take her to her father's house or have him come to mine to watch her while I attended class. I would get home each day by noon, have lunch and then take her to the park until she got tired. We would come upstairs and take a nap. After we woke up, I'd prepare dinner while doing my homework and videotaping her while she entertained herself. This was my routine and one that relieved me from all my worries.

From birthday parties to holiday celebrations to game nights, my apartment was often filled wall-to-wall with family and friends. Monthly and bimonthly party planning became something that kept me entertained during this time. For the first couple of years of my daughter's life, I made it a point to have in-house events because I truly didn't want to lug her out and about. It was also comforting to have created a house many considered home and someplace cozy. It was something I didn't experience in my youth. Growing up, I always went to others' houses, and was always ashamed to bring my friends to my house.

My daughter's first Halloween, Christmas and birthday were made a really big deal and it felt good having everyone come to me. Any and everything that I wasn't able to experience in the short period of time that my mother was alive and not able to provide, I now enjoyed with Star. I vicariously relived my childhood through her, perhaps even enjoying and appreciating it more than she does. I love to see the excitement on her face.

In learning and growing as a parent, I reward her stellar grades with the monetary items that she wants. But most of all, I enjoy the hours, minutes and seconds spent everyday with her because they are precious. Memories are for a lifetime. Time is the one thing we cannot get back. I have enjoyed every stage of her growth and although some stages are more challenging than others, I must say it is pretty amazing to see the changes as she grows. From her first clear word "Daddy," to her teeth coming in, the first tooth coming out to her first step, I didn't miss a beat. The development into the person she wants to be is one that I have learned to allow. Having her do as I say without giving her a voice or to be what and whom I want her to be without giving her a choice is not the method I use. It breaks a child's spirit. Mine had been broken in my youth. Very little love shown, respect and guidance.

One day, we were preparing for church, and she decided she didn't want to wear big, frilly dresses anymore. I simply told her, "As long as it is presentable, by all means, get in them and let's roll." She had on a fancy sweater and a skirt but felt the need to wear her rock star Converses. Had I said something similar in my youth, I would've gotten popped in my mouth, have had to wear what I no longer felt comfortable in and forced to go somewhere I had no desire to go. Hence, the mental block related to what I was taught while in church as a child. Today, I move to the beat of my own drum. Discipline and consistency can make you a better person, but because I was forced in so many instances in my life and not given a choice, now I must be in control and move freely as I please.

Many things are asked of children in shaping them to be upstanding, decent, involved-in-the-world citizens. It helps to allow them some free rein, to allow them to be who they are. My daughter is free-spirited and respectable. She is confident and isn't afraid to approach and take a shot at the unknown.

I remember her first introduction to piano lessons. After day 1, she said, "Mommy, I don't like it." I persuaded her to try more classes. It was a struggle but after a fifth lesson, she was thrilled and I re-enrolled her. She enjoyed the recitals and being the center of attention. She would have her mind set on activities I introduced her to which she really wanted to do, such as dance and playing an instrument. As a trade-off, she would have to participate in an activity that I wanted her to do as well. Giving her that nudge helped her embrace the new without hesitation. I taught my daughter at the age of 8 how to thread a needle and now she practices sewing clothes for her dolls. She has an eye for the arts and design.

A NEW START

My unemployment ran out the day I graduated college. Nobody but God. To be allowed to take care of one thing at a time and succeed at it was a blessing. At times we have it in our minds that we are ready to walk away from a job, person or situation, but then get comfortable again because we lose sight of our goal. God steps in and gives us a little push so that we are then able to see what He has in store for us. Dwelling and staring at the door that just closed too long keeps you from seeing other opportunities. During the year I was out of work, I was able to pull funds from my 401K. I took the tax penalty and paid up my bills for year and survived, using my weekly unemployment check for household needs. As for my school tuition, I had no worries because financial aid covered my undergraduate education. Sometimes losing something you thought was the end all be all can be the best thing that ever happened to you.

I knew that my time of being at home was coming to an end. So it was time to introduce Star to daycare. Going by a friend's referral, I enrolled Star at a day care owned by a woman named Essie called Comfy Places Smiley Faces. Essie was beautifully spirited and nurturing, and Star quickly adjusted. She would unstrap herself from her stroller when we were at the corner near where the daycare center was located and take off running. That was a good sign; she was not often around many others than family, and her response gave me a feeling of comfort.

I had started my job search about two months before I graduated, but hadn't been consistent. For some reason, I figured once I graduated, it would be easier. I was wrong. After graduation, I started creating profiles on various websites, uploaded my resume and applied for jobs daily. I also reached out to friends and my connections in the workforce to see if anyone was hiring. A month after I graduated, I was still out of work and was now beginning to panic because I was running out of money and didn't have anyone to lean on for help.

But blessings seem to come in abundance. It almost seems as if I pray so much and so hard that when they happen, I am overwhelmed with options and left to make decisions based on my wants and needs.

I received a call from two temp agencies, one company and Beth Israel Hospital within one week. I was called to temp at the New York University School of Medicine as a receptionist. I accepted and reported that Monday morning.

My first day at the Development department at NYU School of Medicine was interesting. I met many of the staff and I was paid $12 an hour. The daycare charged more than 50 percent of my weekly pay. My daughter's father agreed to pay her daycare, which helped me a great deal. At times, starting from the bottom is necessary so when you make it to the top or where you want to be you will have a better understanding of the processes from start to finish. I am never too proud and have always been humble.

That week, I also received a call from Beth Israel Hospital to be a program coordinator in the Residency department. The job seemed interesting and like one I knew I could do. But it only offered a salary of $28,000, the same amount of money I made during my last year at Fleet Bank. I had a bachelor's degree now and I deserved more, so I declined. I decided to just focus on the current position at NYU. Overtime, I was confident that I would be made permanent.

As a receptionist, I met some great people. One of the qualities that I love about myself is that I am a people person and a conversationalist. I can engage in a conversation with anyone and discuss various topics.
In my life's journey, I have met many people who were passers-by. However, there was a message and reason for our meeting that I would later find out.

There was one woman who would frequently come to the office to meet with the vice dean. Her name was Leena Greves. I had no idea who she was or the nature of their visit but I would keep her entertained until her meeting time. After about a month of seeing her, she finally introduced herself as the new Executive Director of Operations. I was shocked. She asked if I had been made permanent yet. I responded, "No." She whispered, "Give me some time and you will be." I was ecstatic. Major changes had taken place in the department and I had been asked to cover the lines of the Vice Dean and to help with projects until another assistant was hired. It was interesting working for someone with so many obligations and demands. I learned to manage her calendar as well as other projects that came my way. Leena would coach me as projects came. Once an assistant was hired, I was made permanent to assist the Director of Development and Operations. The turnover for the assistant position was high. Throughout my two years there, three assistants had come and gone. I would sit in and assist where there was a need until a rehire came.

The experience and knowledge gained can never be taken from me, so although I was not paid to perform duties beyond my job description, the more I learned the more I would be able to use in future positions. The biggest challenge was learning how to directly work for someone with a high title and demands. High demands at times came with a trickle-down, domino effect of high stress levels and attitudes.

I was engrossed in work with the many opportunities presented, then one day, after about a year of being at her daycare, Star begged me not to take her. She cried, but would not tell me why. Because neither she nor I was sick, I decided to go into work and would just leave and take a personal day if whatever was going on with Star became a problem, or if having her at work with me was an issue.

I didn't want to put Star on the spot in front of her day care provider, so on the way there I asked why did she not want to go. "Did someone touch or hurt you? Are you scared?" She simply replied, "Mommy, I just wanted to take the train and go to work with you."

Star has that gift of truly knowing what to do or say to get my full attention even today. I realized then that a lot of what she had been use to had ceased. I was now too mentally overwhelmed to run in the park with her, for example. So I opted to make sure to create time for coloring, painting, reading books and watching movies.

****

After a year, things were beginning to look up and my need for more convenience in my life became more apparent. I wanted a car. I decided to look online for options and then went to visit a dealer. I walked in and a silver Nissan caught my eye. It was perfect inside and out. I instantly saw myself driving it. I didn't think it was possible because I didn't have much money and didn't have a long credit history. But all was made possible and I drove out that day. I was very nervous and decided to go pay my grandmother a visit so that she could show me how to pump gas. Or just provide some moral support.

Since I had gotten my license two years prior, I had done very little driving. One day, a good friend, Leo, came by around the time I had gotten off work and picked me up from the train station, and I boldly asked if I could drive us to pick up my daughter from daycare. He said, "Sure." I took the wheel like a champ. But I was nervous and I asked him if he was. He said, "Why do you ask? I know you can do it." Another time I drove was when my cousin Janet asked me to watch her daughter Kari and she left her car with me. I was nervous, but challenged myself and took it for a spin and was happy with the results. That same summer we were heading up to her friend Ciara's house in Poughkeepsie for a backyard barbecue and she had asked me to drive. I felt pressure because of the length of the drive and the fact that I had my cousin Chastity and my daughter in the car. When I made it, I just let out a long sigh. So while it was indeed convenient to have a car, I wasn't confident in my driving skills because I had very little experience and it wasn't within my means. Still, the car became a belated graduation gift. It has been nine years and it's paid off and I still have my baby today. It was my first and as long as it has no problems, parting with it is not necessary.

****

While working at NYU, one of my dearest co-workers opened my heart, mind and eyes to unconditional friendship and became one of my closest friends. Her name is Deanna Morris. Within the first three months of having my car, I had major problems. The issues were being corrected, but the dealership was all the way in suburban Yonkers. It was time to pick the car up, and as I headed to work that morning, I was trying to figure out how I would be able to get to the dealership before it closed. The day before, I had been in conversation with Deanna, randomly speaking about this issue.

I was one train station away from going under the tunnel to get to work when I received a phone call from Deanna. She quickly explained that she had taken the day off and if I needed her to pick up my car, she could do it. I was speechless. She went on to tell me that she could drive my car and park at my daughter's daycare center and leave my key in my daughter's coat pocket. I had a few seconds before I would lose phone service on the train to make a decision. So, I hesitantly accepted. I had never had someone take control of a situation with a plan. I was nervous because although she seemed nice and we talked and took the train home daily, I trusted no one and kept everyone at a distance.

I threw myself into projects that day to avoid thinking of the "what if's" then I got the call that she was on her way to get my car and that she needed me to call the dealership to alert them. Soon after, I received another call that she had parked my car and had left the key with my daycare provider as planned. I was in awe and beyond grateful.

There aren't many people who would go out of their way to help someone in need as she had done or I would. It has been 10 years and her stripes have never changed. In fact, I have met her family and they are just as awesome. I look forward to visiting her family even without her present.

That day when she picked up my car goes down in history as the first day I allowed myself to look at people differently. Not everyone is out to hurt me. I still remain cautious, but she will always have a very special place in my heart and life. As I write this, one of my favorite songs, "Count on Me" by Whitney Houston and CeCe Winans from the *Waiting to Exhale* soundtrack just came on. Perfect moment in time.

I had spent two years at NYU, with little opportunity to grow in this department, and I felt that I was ready to move on and take on projects with greater meaning. To be engaged where there was room to make a difference would satisfy my need to feel accomplished. My cousin Janet had reached out to me about an opening at her job for an administrative assistant. I went in for the interview and found that it was a fit for what I knew I could do and wanted to do. I would assist in the recruitment process at Spence, an Independent all-girls school that went from grades K-12. The position definitely peaked my interest. It was part-time where I would only work from August through February, but the hourly rate was high. So my plan and goal was to save money, and during the months I wasn't working and was collecting unemployment, I could go back to school for my master's degree. I was confident that with my performance and experience, I would soon be considered for a full-time position. So, I accepted the position and went on faith.

The atmosphere within the educational sector was empowering. Having my hands in something that would affect another's growth was exceptionally rewarding to me.

Coming in during the summer months, before recruitment began, to get acclimated to the system and process was necessary and very beneficial. I was able to see the process from the very beginning to the end. I like to make sense of a project before carrying it out. The recruitment process was similar to that of my daughter's being tested and getting into her private school. Parents are first interviewed and then children are put in a room with other children where they are graded on how they interact, behave and on their basic knowledge of the alphabet, shapes, images and sounds. There weren't many spots to offer each year, so it was highly competitive.

I was grasping the concepts of my duties and familiarizing myself with the software. The part of my degree I enjoyed the most was navigating the computer and Web design. I can navigate any computer program and database systems quickly. Being computer savvy made my on boarding less complicated. Additional training on the database required me to travel to Boston for a few days. I was thrilled with the opportunity, but not being able to see my daughter for that many days would have its effect on me.

I had taken my first trip away from my baby to Miami as a graduation gift to myself and drinks were a must to keep my mind off of missing her. I enjoyed myself, but my days seemed much longer than I wanted them to be.

When I took the business trip to Boston, Star had just begun pre-kindergarten at the private school at which she had interviewed and been accepted. I had asked her father to take care of her in my absence and all was confirmed. Now I was prepping to get through the training course and back home to her. I took her to school and was on the highway headed north right after. It was about a four-hour drive, and it was an experience because I had never really driven alone that far of a distance. I don't quite remember how much of a nuisance I was, but I am sure I called home often to make sure she was OK. I do the same today. That is my baby, and at this stage, I am certain I won't change.

The training classes and activities were fun and Boston reminded me of the South. The people were nice, and it was less crowded than New York with reasonably priced property. But after four days there, I was so ready to come home to my baby. The return trip home seemed faster and I went straight to pick up my baby. I had to make up for lost time.

Within a week of my return, my baby's skin started reacting to something like I had never seen before. She had eczema, but this was different.

Within a month, my world started turning upside-down. I experienced all of the following mentally and emotionally. My ship became rocky, approaching heavy waves that I could see from a distance, but with very little strength to control the ship's direction.

I felt tremors akin to ones I imagined were like those from earthquakes experienced in California, and which shook my apartment and knocked everything I had crashing to the floor. My vision became blurred, my hearing faded and my heart's bandages had slipped off because of the amount of additional energy and pumping of blood needed just to get by. I felt like all my wounds were exposed.

I had finally come to a place in my life where I couldn't handle any other trials and needed the strength from my Father in Heaven to be my rock. I surrendered to my Father because losing the one life that I gave life to would put me in between four padded walls or worse, because life would have no meaning.

ALMOST LOST STAR—MADE A BELIEVER

Star was in her second month of school when she came from school with three red bumps in perfect alignment as if she had been lying down on something unsanitary. One on her cheek, arm and leg. I asked her a few questions, and both she and the paraprofessional in her class confirmed that she had slept on a mat without sheets.

Star's teacher was away on maternity leave and no teacher had been assigned in her absence. I was concerned as most parents were. I took Star to see her allergist, Dr. Jean Lake, and got a topical cream for her skin. The blemishes went away.

A short time later, Star fell while running in the house and nicked her knee. I cleaned it with peroxide. The next day I noticed a little swelling, but I thought it was due to the impact of her fall. So I monitored it. The day after that, she had a limp and more swelling, so I rushed her to the Children's Hospital at Montefiore. Because of the MRSA bacteria scare, which was a main topic on the news, she was admitted almost immediately after a culture was taken. An orthopedic surgeon and dermatologist examined her. Pus was drained from her knee and the swelling went down. Star was discharged a few days later. She was diagnosed as having Cellulitis and sent home with a prescription for Bactrim that she was to take for the next 14 days. On the 12th day, she developed a fever and became very fatigued. I was able to bring the fever down by giving her Motrin, but on the evening of the 14th day, the fever came back. I planned to take her to her primary pediatrician the following day. By the time we woke up, Star's eyes were crusted together and her fever was back. I applied Vaseline to her eyes and used a wet cloth to assist with opening them. Her eyes were a little pink, so I assumed she had pink eye. We arrived at the clinic as a walk-in at 8a.m. Star's doctor wasn't in, so we saw another.

Star would not open her eyes, and she was dehydrated. The doctor said it appeared to be a viral infection. She advised me to take her home and give her lots of liquid and Motrin. I had given her Motrin for two days already without much change, so I was very reluctant to give her more. So, the doctor said to come back the next day if she worsened.

We returned home. I tried giving Star liquids, along with Tylenol for her fever, but she was disinterested and went to sleep. When she awoke three hours later, her fever was down, but her eyes were still pink, and now her lips were beginning to swell and dark red, almost burgundy-colored, bumps began appearing on her arms and scalp. She went to the bathroom and screamed that her urine burned.

Star's condition was quickly changing for the worse. I decided to rush her to the emergency room, and she was admitted almost immediately. Doctors poked and probed and took a biopsy to try to determine what was wrong. After much poking, prodding and taking a biopsy, doctors determined that Star had had an allergic reaction to the Bactrim and had developed Stevens-Johnson syndrome, a rare skin disorder.

The condition was so rare doctors at the Children's Hospital at Montefiore were unfamiliar with the illness and its treatment. So, initially, the priority was to keep my daughter hydrated. She was still running a fever and her father and I opted to have doctors put her on steroids and to give her morphine to help with the pain of her skin blistering.

Specialists from every area—dermatology, infectious diseases, optometry, gynecology—examined Star. Stevens-Johnson attacks the skin, eyes, mouth and genital area. Star's face was swollen, blistered and distorted. She was drooling because she could not close her mouth. The whites of her eyes were black and blisters on her body that had been red were now brown. She appeared to have been burned from head to toe. I didn't recognize my baby. I did everything I could to keep her away from seeing her reflection in the mirror attached to her food tray.

On the fourth day of her hospitalization, the doctors came into her room with a look of lost hope and said there was nothing else they could do for her. They were in the process of looking for another bed on another floor in the intensive care unit. I broke down and cried. I just wanted to take the pain away from her. What I would have given to be able to just lie there and endure the painful burning sensations for her. Just as many wanted to do for me when I was lying in pain recovering as a child. That became my story as this one had now become hers.

I slept in the bed next to her day in and day out. I had no appetite. I barely ate or slept. My grandmother had checked into a rehab center nearby during this time, and I made it a point to pull myself together enough to spend an hour or two with her. I didn't share what was going on. But after a third visit, she asked where Star was. I told her she was with her father, but my grandmother knows me well. I would never be without my baby for too long. I broke down and she held me and demanded I tell her what was going on. She took the news well, but was as worried as I.

Later that day, doctors came into Star's room with a look of hope. They shared that a bed had become available in the intensive care unit at New York's Cornell medical center, which specialized in burn cases and major skin issues.

God knew His children were suffering. Life and my faith had been slowly slipping away from me and He stepped in. An on-time God He is.

Everything happened so fast. Star was immediately taken by ambulance to Cornell. Her father and I followed in our cars. I was a nervous wreck and emotionally done, but knew I had to be strong for my baby. I worried about how Star might react if she awoke and was in an unfamiliar place with no one she knew. I rushed inside the hospital without parking my car. I left the keys in the car, pointed to the valet employee to park it and took off running.

I literally ran upstairs to my baby's room. Due to the high contagion factor, everyone, including staff, had to wear masks and gowns to protect us and Star. But I walked into her room, and everyone was all smiles. The staff told me about all the things Star had told them about herself and her family during the ambulance ride, things like her full name and the fact that she and I lived alone in the Bronx.

My heart was beating so loud and fast I could hear it. When I got close enough to Star to kiss her, she was unconscious again. I wanted her to wake up and talk to me. But Star's turnaround period had begun. She no longer had fevers. Her lesions started to dry and the dead skin fell away. It was clear that Cornell knew how to treat this illness.

Star's room was perfect and serene. It overlooked the East River and FDR Highway. I would read to her, give her as many kisses as I could, and just talk to her. Then I would sit at the window and stare at the river waters and passing cars.

I often wondered if anyone other than myself had endured the hurt and pain that I had in this lifetime. Hours would past and I would be in the same spot hoping and wishing. I finally broke down and did something that I never thought I would do. I got down on my knees on the germy hospital floor (although it's probably cleaner than most places) and prayed through my tears that my baby would wake up for me. I just wanted to hear her voice again. I knew the staff had said she had spoken to them, but I hadn't heard her voice in days. Which felt like forever.

As God himself is my witness, I got up off my knees and sat at the window. After a few minutes, I heard my baby call out my name. She said, "Mommy, can you bring that balloon over to me and then read the book you were reading to me every night." I was speechless and my eyes filled with tears because I couldn't believe that all it took was for me to bow down and ask for what I wanted. Most people only notice God when they are going through something and find themselves in that position. I was so overjoyed. I did exactly what she said and tried to control my cries as I read to her. My prayers had been answered within seconds. From that moment, I realized that God is always on time and HE gives us exactly what we ask for in his time. HE knew I was at the end of my rope and was at another weak point in life when I was expected to be strong.

Friends, family, classmates, her principal, her daycare provider, had all come by faithfully to support Star and me. Star's grandfather

Devon and grandmother Carol would pray over her often. They are strong believers and there was no worry on their faces when they came to visit. They knew it was just a matter of time and this, too, shall past. When prayers go up, blessings definitely come down.

Star's nurses came in and were thrilled that she had awakened. There were hugs all around. The medical staff had gone above and beyond the call of duty, which helped us get through that horrific experience.

Words couldn't express my gratitude. Through this experience of seeing my daughter in a deformed state, with tons of blood, and staying in the hospital with her the whole time, God had truly answered my "how" questions and made me see my own strength. Having lost so many people before, I probably would have been taken out if I had lost my baby too.

From that moment, I was able to identify and appreciate more of the little things that mattered in life. I was tested and God had answered the question, "How would I manage if there were a situation in which my child got hurt or needed me?" It was the first day of a new life for me.

Star continued to make progress in her ability to eat, her activity level and her overall healing. Family and friends spent Thanksgiving that year by her bedside. By Star's 11th day in the hospital, doctors examined her and said she would be discharged soon.

Since Star would be coming home within days, I decided to go home to clean and disinfect.

In Star's room, I grabbed all her teddy bears and placed them in her hammock. She had been diagnosed with asthma when she was 3, along with dirt, dust and mold allergies, which contributed to her asthma. Having teddy bears that collect dust was a problem, but I didn't immediately get rid of them because she loved them so much. I placed them in a hammock with hopes she would outgrow her allergies.

There was one teddy bear that she particularly loved and always wanted to carry everywhere we went. So I had to constantly wash it when she wasn't paying attention. Star felt it was wrong to put her teddies in the washing machine. One day she even asked if I would do that to her. "Of course not," I said. "Why would you do it to my teddy?" she replied." You hurt their bodies, they get dizzy and besides it is too dark in there." Star was always a sensible child. After her enlightenment, I would just take them and wash them when she was not paying attention, and put them back before she started missing them. All were her favorite but only a few got to travel, eat and sleep with her.

I came upon the favorite of the month and noticed it had bandages all over the body from head to toe. I sat down to observe the bear. The bandages were all different colors and characters. I leaned back on my bed as I realized this was Star's way of expressing herself. "Oh my goodness," was all I could say. My baby had been in tons of pain while at home taking the meds and didn't tell me. I felt like the worst parent for not paying attention. Why did she not tell me? We talk about everything. Her illness had been due to an allergic reaction to the medication taken to get over the MRSA. But in hindsight, it was a blessing to have finished the medicine and go through the process and survive. Especially seeing as how this was the only cure, as I was told.

Her experience will be the story of her life and it is important for her to remember. She is a survivor of something others may not have been as lucky to overcome.

After her discharge from the hospital, we returned to the doctor over the following months to ensure that her recovery continued and that she was out of the woods. Finally, her vision completely cleared and other than some blotchy patches on her skin, Star received a clean bill of health.

Going back to school presented a few challenges. While Star's face had fully cleared, her arms and legs remained scarred. She didn't want to wear sweaters or long-sleeved tops, and I didn't want her to be teased and have her feelings hurt. So we talked about it. I told her that her spots made her special and showed her spots on my body, as well as told stories about pretty animals with spots. Star was not bothered by her scars. After a few years, they faded and blended into her normal skin tone. She said she missed them and wished she had them back.

Similar to the scarring of my childhood, symbolizing life and God's grace.

I had not been at work since my daughter's illness. There hadn't been enough strength in my body. I had felt lifeless and mentally incapable of functioning. Staying busy had always been my coping method, but not this time. I had had a one-track mind. No one and nothing mattered except the survival of my baby.

I returned to the all-girls school, and realized I wanted a position where I would have more hands-on involvement. The director and I discussed a position I was interested in, but it didn't pan out.

So, I spent my days volunteering at my daughter's school. I helped with arts and crafts, read the children stories and helped prepare their in-class meals. When I pick my daughter up it's so nice to hear the other children say, "Hello, Star's mom."

Star made new friends and so did I. One was a little girl named Arianna Hayes, who remains Star's best friend today. I met a crying Arianna, upset over her mom having dressed her in a sweat suit. "My mommy forgot that it was not a gym day and I have on my sweat suit," she said through tears. I looked at her and whispered to her that she was special and that it was OK. I could relate to this moment and thought that as parents at times we have so much going on in our lives it is impossible to remember everything. I later had the pleasure of meeting her mother, Leandra Morgan, while chaperoning a class trip. We shared so many things in common, including how much our girls mean to us. Leandra is another person who lives in my heart forever and always.

During my time off, I spent time at Star's school, rearranged my apartment, did some reading and became bored with not working. And if I were to go back to school for my master's degree, quite frankly, I had no idea what I was interested in studying.

But I had learned that plans do not always work out the way I want them to as God may have other plans for me. I may not understand in the moment, but in due time, it all makes sense.

I have always felt that God has a sense of humor and sits on His throne laughing and shaking His head at me while I am running around trying my hardest to do things I want to do in the way that I want to do them. Or despite the curve balls thrown my way that tested my strength, patience and faith. He sits back and waits until I have exhausted all possibilities and have sat down before the answer is revealed after coming to Him. God wants our undivided attention all the time. He wants to be our everything. The moment that I started to consult with Him before every decision, life and everything and everyone in it became alive. The good, bad and indifferent were more visible. I no longer had tunnel vision but now a vision of my Heavenly Father.

I started my job search again, landing a temp job at a bank. But I continued to search, and my hunt landed me back at NYU, this time in the Department of Pediatrics Residency Program. I had stopped by my old Development office to say hello, and ended up chatting with my old boss, the Operations Director, Leena. When she learned that I was looking for a job, she made a phone call to human resources, which led to my placement with Pediatrics. That was the start of my blessings flowing.

It wasn't long before I was promoted to the position of residency coordinator. The job that I prayed for was challenging. I was responsible for the day-to-day needs of 56 medical residents. Having the hands-on experience and building relationships with my residents were just for me. There were days when I was expected to be at work by 7:30 a.m. and didn't leave, at times, until 12 hours later. There was travel to different states for retreats. I became a better organizer, communicator and multitasker. My patience had increased. I had gained confidence, and last but not least, the ability to know when enough is enough and when to take a back seat to rest and focus on the next goal.

My job overflowed into my personal life. Star's father was a great help to me. I needed him to take her to school and pick her up when need be. I endured the sacrifice of not having my daughter home with me some nights but instead at her grandmother's where I would go to tuck her in and kiss her. But I had a world of determination and was sure that one day I would master it all and walk away with a smile.

I recently re-enrolled in school and stepped down to the position of program coordinator, a job that offers me much more flexibility, allowing me time to do what I need to do. It's the best decision that I've made in years. I am grateful to have had the opportunity to perform at the capacity I did over the past three years. I have learned from and trained many through sharing all of what I have gained over the years.

Star's father has been very consistent on this ride with me. It is what I needed to succeed, achieve and make money to take care of my household. Most would say this is what a man is supposed to do to support his child, and that's true. However, the majority of men do not. When a relationship is over, some men walk away from the mother of their child and create a whole new family. Child support is good and is needed to take care of your child, but if there is no personal relationship being built, the child suffers. Whatever shortcomings her father has, his physically being there for her has had a great impact. Star's and her father's relationship and bond have only gotten stronger. She is well balanced and secure within herself, free-spirited and outgoing. He is her king and she is his princess.

THE STRESS OF LOSS

With all that I had experienced regarding Star's life-threatening crisis, it got me thinking about the fact that we're all on borrowed time and will be called home when God is ready for us. Before the death of my mom, I had had absolutely no concept of death. Then my mother died, and I subsequently experienced having death wipe out most of my immediate family, leaving the kids behind to cope and survive.

- My grandpa Johnny Beaken, to whom we were very close when Mommy was alive, died about two years after she did. My mother was his first-born, and he took her death hard.
- Grandma Meena's younger sister Aunt Donna died soon after we arrived in New York.
- Grandma Meena's father died within a couple years of his daughter Aunt Donna.
- Uncle Bob passed on right before Aunt Mira.
- Despite the number of deaths that had occurred up to this point, they didn't prepare me for this loss. Death claimed Aunt Mira, my everything. I died again.
- Two years later, Aunt Deidre died violently, reminding me of the way violence led to my mother's death.
- Grandma Flore suffered from diabetes and after many years of pain was called home. She finally let go after having met her great-grandchildren.
- Great-grandma Ann, my grandmother Meena's mother, had her homegoing.
- Then Uncle Ben, Grandma Meena's brother.
- Most recently, my aunt Margaret passed away. She gave me the push I needed to complete this book. In her last days, I was happy to have achieved this goal.
- Death even came at me via the death of a very close friend Donald, who at the age of 15 was shot to death. His death was too close to home and made me realize that death didn't discriminate with regard to age. I remember the cab ride to the funeral home, bumping Lauryn Hill's "Killing Me Softly." To this day, I can't help but turn that song off when I hear it.

Through all these tragedies, Grandma Meena appeared strong, but she began to slowly lose it, even suffering a mild stroke around the time of the death of her father. She was never good about expressing how she felt. Instead, she internalized everything, and the effects were worse than one would expect.

While death is the one sure thing that we will all face, knowing this doesn't make it easier to cope or prepare for a loss. The many deaths I've experienced have opened old wounds and sparked flashbacks. The only face I see in a casket is always a glimpse of my mother's face. I rarely attend funerals because of this, and when I do, I sit as far away from the casket as possible.

Despite the immense pain I felt in my weakest moments after my aunt Mira died, even to the point of contemplating suicide, none of that compares with the pain my grandmother Meena was suffering.

She lost most of her immediate family within two years of one another over a span of 10 to 20 years. Her biggest challenge was keeping it together as she took on the responsibility of raising my brother and me.

And as the losses piled on, my grandmother began to drink more, harming herself and others. She would get so drunk, she'd lose her balance and end up hurting herself or becoming defensive and start hitting someone else. That violent fight between her and my uncle that I had walked in on started because she had been antagonizing him while she was intoxicated. There was definitely no justification for my uncle to reacting the way that he did toward his mother. However, with his mental state and not taking his medication as prescribed, she became a threat and an enemy to him.

I remember the night in the hospital with her and the many requests I made to have her counseled. I inquired about programs that would help her with her alcohol abuse. After a two-day stay in the hospital, I received a phone call at work from the nurse letting me know that she had been evaluated. She had been found to be in her right mind, had refused any additional help and would be released that day. I was furious. She was like an out-of-control, unruly child. The things she did when I wasn't around pissed me off.

Once I got a phone call from someone who lived near her, informing me that she had hit a man in the back of his head with a bottle. No reason. I just knew she had probably been drinking. It scared me because when she sobered up, she wouldn't remember what she did while intoxicated. On many occasions, she would be scared for her life once she became sober and was harassed as she walked the streets by people she had taunted when she was drunk.

One other time, she was at the corner store and got into an altercation with a female customer. During the heated discussion, my grandmother slapped the women and called her outside to continue the fight. Police called me to give warning. They were tired of my grandmother's behavior and threatened to arrest her if she continued. I was frustrated and I couldn't control her behavior or baby-sit her while I was at work or school.

She frequently walked around with open beer cans, which would earn her a ticket. But she would curse out the police, get violent and end up in jail with a fine for disorderly conduct. I would get that call from the jail in the middle of the morning, day or night call that she needed me to come get her.

One summer day, I was sitting in the cul-de-sac of the projects, waiting for her to come outside, and noticed a police van on the other side of the street. A short time later, a cop started walking toward me. I was nervous because of my fear of cops, but knew I had done nothing wrong. The officer was young, black and handsome, and he smiled as he neared. We exchanged hellos. Before he could say another word, my grandmother came out in her pajamas and flip-flops screaming, "Get away from my granddaughter! She doesn't like or want you. She doesn't need a cop in her life!" He laughed and asked if she was my grandmother. I replied yes, and he smiled and said, "Have a nice day." My grandmother then says, "Wait, you can have me though." Then, she lifted up her pajama top, exposing her breast lying flat on her waistline. I was so embarrassed. The police officer thought it was the funniest thing ever. He continued to laugh while walking away.

My grandmother went in and out of the hospital after falling or due to someone hitting her back in defense against her. I started to realize the pattern in her behavior as a need for my attention. During birthdays, holidays, family events or when I had friends over to my house, she would make an appearance and show out or I would receive a phone call about her, which would pull my attention away from whatever I had been doing.

Once, my grandmother got so drunk she passed out on a corner near her home. Some children saw her and called the ambulance. I usually paid my grandma a visit at least two to three times a week. I normally called for her from the street and waited for her response. If she didn't respond—maybe her music was too loud or she was asleep—I would leave and try again the next day. This time around, when I didn't get her on the second or third day, I began to get worried and asked around to see if anyone had seen her. She frequently lost her keys and had to change her locks often so the spares I had never worked.

Someone told me she had been taken to Bellevue Hospital after assaulting a cop. Another told me she was taken to the hospital because she had fallen. Bellevue is affiliated with NYU, where I worked, so I decided to start my search there. But there was no information on file about her. I then called other hospitals with no success. After three days, I filed a missing person report with the police. Finally, a lawyer I was dating at the time made a few phone calls and found out that she was in a hospital, one that I had called but had been given the runaround.

When I arrived at the hospital, my grandmother was so happy. "I told you she would find me," she screamed out to the nurses.

She was so weak and seemed to have lost weight. My grandmother is 5 feet tall and 98 pounds or less, wet. She looked much thinner than that. The nurses explain that she had been detoxing and that her limbs were too weak for her to return home right away. They recommended she be moved to a rehabilitation center.

I was elated. Finally, she would be monitored, restricted from the outside world and from the inner pains and demons that haunted her. She was assigned to a rehabilitation nursing home where she stayed for the next six months. I made it a point to support her and visit at least twice a week and on the weekends even though I had to care for my daughter when she was hospitalized as well. Overtime Grandma Meena grew stronger and started to remind me of the woman I had known when I was much younger. While in rehab was one of the first times she held me and told me she loved me. I was 27. Better late than never.

I remember wanting to hear that the day I sat down with her after earning my Bachelor of Science degree and reiterated all my achievements and expressed how I felt after all the years of hurtful things she had said to me. I yearned to hear, "I love you," or "I am proud of you." Instead, it struck a nerve and she cursed me out, and then kicked me out of her house.

Growing up, what I heard daily was:

- I would never amount to anything and wouldn't graduate high school. To impress and please her, I graduated high school and earned my undergraduate degree, then went back to pursue my master's.
- "So what, I had my license by 16," she would say. To prove myself, I went out and got my permit, license and then bought a car.

She said I would end up like my mother and have a baby at a young age. I didn't get pregnant until many years later. I moved out and demonstrated that I was independent and responsible by never returning home. I wanted so much to impress her. To make her proud of me and to love me as the only parent I had and the one who took care of me in my mother's absence should. I know my grandmother loved me, but because she wasn't given the love she needed from her parents, she didn't know how to give or express it.

****

A few months before the hospital stay that ended in rehab, a particularly ugly incident happened. I had taken my grandmother and daughter out to eat at New Roc City, an entertainment complex just north of the city. I wanted to show my grandmother another side of life. She loves the little brick building she resides in and often feels she'll miss something or will be missed if she leaves for too long. My grandmother was a little tipsy, but not to a point that I thought would cause me any embarrassment.

We get to the restaurant, and she begins flirting with the waiters and cracking jokes. Because she doesn't go out much, we agreed to order her the only thing she recognized on the menu: chicken, mashed potatoes and broccoli. I had no idea what was coming next.

After ordering, my grandma stood up and said, "Why did you bring me around these white people? They don't like us." She began walking to the white people's tables, taunting them. I was so embarrassed.

My grandmother returned to our table, and the waiter arrived with our food. I had lost my appetite and asked the waiter for a container to pack it up in hopes of avoiding another scene. Star was hungry and began eating while we waited for my container. Grandma pushed her food across the table, slamming it into the condiments, shouting, "What the f*ck is this? I don't want this sh*t. I said I wanted chicken!" I was so disgusted and didn't care if she ate or if my money went to waste.

The waiter came over with the "to go" containers, and said we had to go. As the wait staff and I packed the food, I avoided making eye contact with my grandmother or responding to her comments. When people are losing their cool, it's often a cry for attention. My ignoring her just made her angrier and she started hitting below the belt.

"There is something I always wanted to tell you," she said, demanding that I look at her when she speaks to me when I continued to avoid her. A huge part of me still felt like that respectful little girl who had to listen. Once our eyes met, she said, "I never liked you and I should have let you die when I had the chance. I paid the nurses to get you back on your feet so we could come back to New York. I should have let you die."

Her voice was so low, her eyes dark and evil. My space was closing in on me. It was getting harder to breathe. Everything around me started to move in slow motion. I saw her lips moving, but heard nothing else. Everything around me went silent. I was in a trance and the only thing that snapped me out of it was my baby girl saying, "Mommy, Mommy, Mommy, I'm finished" as she shook my arm.

I quickly grabbed my food, my daughter and walked out, leaving my grandmother behind. Anger started to set in. I headed to the parking garage.

"Mommy, we cannot leave Grandma here," my daughter said. I couldn't say anything to my 4-year-old. All I knew was that the level of embarrassment and hurt didn't compare to the pain from the knife that I had just pulled out of my heart now that the numbness was wearing away. My grandmother was right on my heels, cursing and screaming. My daughter repeated what she had said about not leaving her. So I decided that because we were some ways away from home, I would get her home in one piece and then leave her alone.

We all got in the car and I turned on the music to drown her out. "I will f*ck you up. Keep playing with me," she said. The little girl who was sitting in the restaurant was left right there. All of the respect I had went out the window and I simply replied, "It's because of Star that you are in my car. You are not going to f*ck me up so shut the f*ck up until you get the hell out."

She shut up for a little while until we were near her house. I let her out on the corner near her building. She got out then slammed and kicked my car door as I sped off.

My daughter had fallen asleep by the time I got home. I was relieved because I had never cried in front of her. The first time she saw me cry was at my friend Clarissa's mom's funeral and she was 6. I was filled with so many emotions and didn't know what to do. A phone call came in and interrupted my thoughts. Ironically, it was Clarissa. While talking to her, I just broke down, right on the phone. For years, I planned my cries. I would do it in the comfort of my own home after hours when all was quiet. Being the oldest and told to be strong for the little ones under me had shaped my thinking and emotions. On the phone with Clarissa, I cried so much, the words couldn't come out. I didn't see or speak to my grandmother again until months later when I received the phone call that she was in the hospital.

After leaving the hospital, my grandmother stayed in rehab for six months. She hadn't craved beer or liquor. She had regained weight and made many friends in the program. She had even managed to meet a man who grew to love her and ended up proposing with a ring. Their time in rehab together kept both of them alive and excelling in the goals and challenges of getting well enough to leave.

After leaving the facility, she agreed to attend adult daycare, where she could spend time with others her age and get her meals for the day. But her commitment only lasted two weeks. One day, the drivers contracted to take her to the program called me to say that she was a no-show. I went to see my grandmother after work to find out what had happened. She said she was no longer interested in being around "sick" people and that she could feed herself. She immediately started drinking again. I was crushed. I felt that all the effort and energy I had put in this time and all the times before were unappreciated.

****

One day, a friend called to tell me that my grandmother hit a young man, and in the resulting fight, got laid out and was waiting for me to come take her to the hospital.

It was in that instant that I realized how fed up I was. Instead of jumping to her beck and call, I asked if they could call an ambulance and then let me know what hospital she would be in. I didn't have the nerves or the strength to see her in the flesh or to deal with her situation. I decided to focus on my daughter's birthday weekend instead.

The guy I was dating at the time disagreed with how I handled it. He had met my grandmother and knew how she was, but felt that no one should hit an older woman, especially a drunken one. That's true, and usually how I get sucked in. However, times and generations have changed and it is hard trying to convince someone under the influence to be mindful of others and to stay to themselves. Their defenses are at a high and nothing said matters.

She would come running to my house telling me someone was chasing her with a gun, but that she didn't know who it was or why. When she was drunk she wouldn't have any recollection of the havoc she caused. Now she was subjecting me to her outside drama, bringing it to my door and jeopardizing my life. I have come to realize that others have brought on most of the issues in my life, not me. I've never been interested in street hustlers or hung out with groups of sh*t starters. If I have beef, I handle it myself on the spot. Any other way puts others' lives at risk.

Crime and random death seem to be at a high nowadays. Life has evolved so much that a prayer is needed every day for your and your family's safety. You don't even have to go outside to be at risk. People get shot just sitting in their house watching television due to stray bullets and street beef. I was standing next to a woman at a summer barbecue and found out a few days later she had been shot and killed while walking home from the store with her son. I was devastated. Now her son will be affected by what he witnessed for the rest of his life because of idiotic, reckless behavior. More parents are burying their children than usual. Kids are not making it out of high school these days. This generation is lost and disturbed and not getting enough of what they need to be productive and respectful citizens. The impact of peer pressure and the resulting copycat events is enough to make you want to live in a bubble and home school your children.

Shootings take place in areas most would not expect and at an hour when many are vulnerable. A gunman entered a school and chose to shoot and kill the many children and teachers in his path. Why? One will never know one's state of mind. It was a complete shocker when shots were fired and death occurred around 9 in the morning at one of New York's most popular tourist locations, the Empire State Building. Even worse, a mother's body was dismembered by her son and stuffed in a garbage bag.

We wake up and don't know how our day will end. Once upon a time, the struggle was to survive and be all that you could be. Today, we struggle, literally, to survive and avoid stray bullets and being in the wrong place at the wrong time.

We never know what is on the minds of people. Chemical imbalance in the brain can happen at any time. A chemical change can take place and a person becomes different if the wrong buttons are pushed. Some people are better at controlling their emotions than others. But there may be dormant feelings that can come alive when least expected.

Hence, my grandmother's behaviors can get her killed. Not everyone will take factors such as her age, gender or the seriousness—or lack thereof—of the situation at hand.

The mind is a powerful and a terrible thing to waste. Losing my mind is a fear of mine. Many in my family suffer from mental disorders that require medication. God knows I have seen my share and should be popping pills for many reasons, but HE keeps me.

****

My daughter's family was having a reunion in Jamaica, and she and I were getting ready to go. It was the day before we were set to leave, and we were getting ready to go visit my grandmother before our trip. As we got dressed, I heard a commotion going on outside my window and then a knock on the door.

It was my neighbor who had come to tell me that there was a woman outside who she thought was my grandmother. An intoxicated woman had stumbled barefoot, her clothes pissy, down the block and fallen and hit her head on the gate in front of my house. I ran downstairs to find my grandmother outside and some of my neighbors on their phones calling 911. I assured them that I would handle it. Once my grandmother saw my face and knew that I was upset, she pulled herself up and refused all help from the neighbors. This was the most wasted that I had ever seen her. I had to lift her up the stairs to my apartment. The most challenging part was keeping her seated because I didn't want her to mess up my furniture and keeping my daughter calm. My daughter loves her grandmother so much, and just like me, wants her to do better. I checked my grandmother for cuts and bruises. She decided against going to the hospital, so after feeding her and finding her a pair of socks and sneakers to wear, I took her home.

She kept saying that we were going to Jamaica to leave her. I tried to explain that it was a vacation and temporary, only to return seven days later from our trip to a disturbing work email regarding her.

A nurse at North Central hospital in the Bronx wrote, asking me to contact her as soon as possible about a Mrs. Meena Beaken. Apparently, while my grandmother couldn't remember my phone number (and had refused to wear the dog tag I had gotten her with my info on it), she did remember where I worked, and the nurse had taken the chance to email me in hopes that I was the right person.

It turned out that while we were away, my grandmother had been drinking, fell, and then needed stitches and staples to fix the cut to her head. I was so upset and afraid to see my grandmother in such a state, it took me a couple of days to go to see her. "What took you so long?" she immediately asked. She was strapped to the bed for fear she would escape. I was so disgusted and responded, "What did you do? I told you I would be out of town. Why do you always get into something and end up in jail or the hospital when I am away or when my attention is needed elsewhere?" She just laughed and said, "OK. Let's go. Get me out of here."

One of the nurses called me into the hall to discuss my grandma's condition, describing her as being "such a beautiful person when she's not drinking," but saying that my grandmother was fighting and screaming during the detox period. "This is one of the reasons she is strapped down," the nurse explained. "Secondly, because you didn't come fast enough for her, we caught her trying to leave one night." The nurse went on to say that my grandmother called my name the whole time, telling them that I would find her and take care of everything because I always do for everyone.

"Do yourself a favor," the nurse counseled. "I know you love her, but start focusing on you and your baby. She will never change, looking at her history here."

Her words brought tears to my eyes. I knew this to be true, but my grandmother was all I had. It was just so hard to truly walk away and leave her to fend for herself.

CREATING MEMORIES – RELIVING MY CHILDHOOD

And so I focused on my baby. Before I had my daughter, I knew very little of the Disney princess. My childhood experience of believing in fairy tales was short-lived. Reality overshadowed it, taking over my dreams and stripping me of hope. Having Star inspired me to explore and experience, for the first time, what many others take for granted.

Given the abuse I had experienced during childhood, I made it a point by the time my daughter was 2 to talk to her about her private areas. About how important it was to tell me if someone touched her. Every day we would go over this, so much so, one day, when I asked if anyone had touched her, she responded, "Yes." I got weak. I was giving her a bath. As calm as I knew how to be, I asked, "Who touched you and where?" She said, "You, Mommy. You just washed my private parts." I felt such relief. From early on, my daughter knew how to make light of moments like this, while still understanding the seriousness.

I wanted to provide my daughter with the kinds of opportunities and experiences I didn't get as a child. From the time she was in the stroller until the present day, we frequently visited the Bronx Zoo and the city's Children's Museum. Seeing the astonished look on my daughter's face when she was introduced to something new was priceless, and accomplishing that became a mission I set out to always complete.

When she was 4, I introduced her to her first plane ride. It was to South Carolina to visit my dad's family. We celebrated Star's fifth birthday down there. It was nice seeing and introducing Star to her aunt, uncles and many cousins. I wanted her to breathe different air and run around barefoot in the grass as I did as a kid. When she asked if she could go outside with no shoes on, I told her "Yes," then I quickly grabbed my camera to capture her expression.

The next year, for her sixth birthday, I put together a princess ball. I was more excited than ever. It was like planning for what I called her "pre-Sweet Sixteen." I took the time to learn the storylines of all the princesses for the girls and superheroes for the boys, and asked everyone to come wearing ballroom dresses and suits. There was karaoke, games and a kids' fashion show where the children were paired up to walk the runway and model for the parents. Star was paired with her first friend, Tyrone, the boy who, when she turned 2 and he was 3, sat down next to her father and told him, "I'm going to marry your daughter when we get older." He is the cutest. On the runway, he wore a crown and gray and pink pinstriped suit, while Star came out wearing a tiara and a light pink dress. She was the prettiest little princess. I know her Sweet Sixteen will be much more elaborate.

During spring break that same year, I flew with Star to San Diego, along with her friend Arianna and mother Leandra. We went to SeaWorld where we saw Shamu and played with the dolphins. We took a nature-themed cruise to Mexico. We got a little sea sick, but it was a great adventure nonetheless. I truly enjoyed the vacations I have with Star by my side, experiencing all that life has to offer.

Just spending quality time with Star is precious. Once we were baking pies together and Star said, "Mommy, I like baking and cooking with you because I get to find out how you are doing and how your day was." I was absolutely taken aback by this and realized that the time and energy I had put into reliving childhood experiences for my own good, but with her, and looking forward to her smile were just part of the joy and fulfillment. Knowing that she also looks forward to these events to learn more about me is priceless! We now make it a point to bake cakes, cookies or pies at least twice a month.

For Star's seventh birthday, we had just moved, and so I surprised her with a bedroom of her own designed like a princess' castle with a "my size" dollhouse and a new bedroom set I knew she would love. I also gave her a hamster (despite my nervousness toward rodents). She did a pretty good job taking care of him, until one night she left him in his exercise ball and he escaped. Star was hurt,

but understood what had happened and said, "God called him to Heaven." I tried to replace it with two other hamsters, but within a two-week span they died, and we were never able to connect with them like we had with the first. I learned a lesson:
Trying to replace something while you are still too emotionally wrapped up in what you lost is not the way to go. Better decisions can be made once you have fully healed and have accepted what happened.

There were so many key qualities involved in child rearing that I missed out on as a child. Not getting enough love, hugs, attention and affection turned me into a person who did not know how to give such things naturally or have the desire to engage in such actions. Although I yearn for love and affection often, I don't seek it and am very selective about who I allow in. The other aspect of quality child rearing is support. By providing a strong support system and guidance, it is your parents, relative or another adult who cares about your well-being that shapes you and your approach to life is different as a result. There are no challenges you don't look forward to. You exude an exalted level of confidence and a better you. Having lacked most, if not all, of these things, I still managed to find my way, but with very little enthusiasm when the prize is won. Having to be my own motivator with a minimal support system contributed to my growth, but it was draining and depressing at times; facing challenges brings me so much anxiety. In some instances, anxiety motivated me, but at times, it sucked my energy.

Life is filled with challenges, but the rewards are to be remembered and celebrated. Best of all, they make you stronger for your next battle. There are times when I rejoiced in great moments for all of a few seconds before being reminded that a storm is usually right around the corner. But often, the good was so all encompassing that it overtook the bad, once arrived, that would have probably destroyed me otherwise.

So, every night, I take about 45 minutes alone to unwind and have a moment from my days. When I was a kid, the bathroom was where I took my solace. Now I walk out on the terrace on nice nights to have my moment. When my daughter was younger, she would knock or just push open the door with a mouth full of words coming out; a story about her day at school that she couldn't wait to tell me about, or a question she feared she'd forget. I accepted the intrusion then, but now, I simply tell her to write her questions down so she won't forget, and to allow me my time. Keeping the lines of communication open is very important to me, and I don't want her to think that I'm not interested in her thoughts. Even when she's being reprimanded, we sit and talk afterward to make sure she is fully aware of her punishment. And even if I don't agree with her, she has the floor to vent. I am hoping that this communication will continue as she gets in her teenage years —but I'm not going to hold my breath. My hopes are that she won't hold things in as I did and internalize. She needs to get things off her chest so she can move forward.

Momma never had the time in her life to tell me there would be days like this. After her death, I always felt like I was thrown out into the frigid ocean with a life jacket, without knowing in which direction to swim because it was too dark to see anything.

In talking with my daughter, I provide the kid-friendly version on some topics, but on many others, I give the raw, uncut version. Life is real, and it is happening much sooner with our children today. I want to be the first to share the good, bad and indifferent in life with my daughter. Again, the foundation of our relationship is built on love and trust. No matter how I feel about the topic she brings to me, we talk about it. The fact that she comes to me with questions means that she heard about it elsewhere and needs clarity and simplification in order to understand. Giving her the support, love and attention she needs is the foundation of what I feel is required to have a strong relationship and to help her become an upstanding, confident citizen ready to take on the world, in my absence.

****

Once during one of my brother's many visits, he insisted that we acknowledge and celebrate Mommy's birthday. It was a big deal. I had never once lit a candle on her day. I had never celebrated or acknowledged anything of my mother's existence because it hurt to relive that time.

I avoid talking about her, celebrating any memories, because I wished what had happened had never occurred or that I could accept what had happened to begin to heal so that I would not hurt as bad. Things would be much different if I hadn't walked in and witnessed it. If only I could simply imagine what had happened to her, perhaps this would lessen the hurt I feel.

But it's funny how God works. The life of my baby was perhaps to fill the hole in my heart around an unforgettable date I had avoided for years. My daughter's due date was on my mother's birthday. My daughter's being born five days earlier was a sign that Mommy is never to be forgotten or replaced, and that to truly be able to live, love and begin to heal and to experience true happiness, Mommy's memory should be revisited, remembered and accepted.

So, my brother and I decided to have a karaoke game night in celebration of our mother. We invited people over and started the evening with karaoke and then played Twister, Scrabble, card games and Wii. There was singing and dancing. My brother made his seafood special, of course making sure not to share his recipe with me. He can definitely get down in the kitchen, having learned how to cook while in jail.

The turnout was beautiful. Our friends and family came and shared in the fun. There were lots of laughs and no drama. It was a success indeed.

****

I don't do well with making year long vacation plans. It will indeed be more economical but the anticipation doesn't happen until the month or week when I am packing. The excitement that I feel making spontaneous movement is more therapeutic for me. It keeps life exciting, focus and looking forward to something great. Long term planning was not as realistic to me.

And so it was with my adventures with Star.

We started going ice-skating. I introduced her to piano and challenged her to try karate while I took kickboxing lessons.

Sometimes, we would spontaneously take a weekend trip. Just quickly packing a bag and food and hitting the highway or getting a last-minute reasonably priced ticket to someplace warm.

We went to Virginia for an extended weekend just to hang out. It was around my brother's birthday, and the trip included him, Grandma Meena, Star, one of Star's best friends and the man in my life at the time. We rode the rides at Kings Dominion, had a barbecue at poolside and a Dave & Buster's game night. This was the first time my brother and I had had a childlike experience of fun together, and we had the time of our lives.

It was during another one of our trips that Star brought the importance of family home. I planned a last-minute trip to Fort Lauderdale, Florida. It was the first time that she and I took a trip out-of-state alone.

It was the most peaceful vacation with my baby. Star and I spent our mornings and afternoons by the pool or at the beach and our evenings having dinner accompanied with entertainment on the strip.

We were having such an enjoyable time, I extended my trip. I asked Star how she felt about extending our trip. The look on her face told me that she was having a good time, but was ready to go home. She said, "Well, I miss my daddy and don't want to stay too much longer."

For a split second, I was confused as to why she was missing him when she saw him every day. We had only been gone for four days. Then, suddenly it made sense. Star's father is a huge part of her day-to-day. I smiled and realized that all of what I didn't have and never experienced, she is blessed to have it all. I absolutely love it. I'm not only introducing and allowing Star to have what I didn't have, but I get to also share in her joy.

When my daughter's prayer for the holidays was to say how happy she was that I had met her father in order to have her, it just warmed my soul.

The word "family" is so strong and powerful. Over the years, I have recruited many friends that I deem as family. My daughter teaches me how important family is when we are away and she has a moment of reflection and says, "Mommy, I miss my daddy." Or at the time when I was looking to relocate and she would simply say, "We can't move too far from our family." Family plays a huge role in her life and if that is the one gift that I can give her by keeping connected, it is one that I am most proud to give and am thankful for it.

It was just like the time Star and I traveled to Jamaica for Star's father's family reunion. I really got to experience the sense of family that I didn't experience as a child. During the flight back home, which was rather bumpy and long, I had time to really take in all that the trip had brought and digest a bit. From the bickering to the making up to the breaking bread together, that is indeed what family is about.

I was familiar with bickering, but in my family, it always led to fighting and eventually someone shedding blood. The one time they all come together is at funerals and even then they can't keep the peace.

For example, I hosted a Halloween party in my apartment for the kids. The house was packed with kids and their parents all dressed in costumes. My grandmother was sipping and I had no idea; my attention was on hosting. She got so wasted; she became angry with her sister and kicked her in the behind. It never failed. One could never just walk away and respect the roof they were under.

Another time my brother and I got into an altercation over some "he say, she say" that caused such a serious wedge in our relationship we didn't speak for years. He allowed a woman to tell him something that I supposedly said that was untrue. He approached me screaming, based in my face and tried to swing. I grabbed for my knife and it was over before it began. He left. And it really got ugly when he realized all his clothes were still in my apartment. (He had been staying with me for a while.) He began banging and kicking on the door. After all the many years of my taking care of him and protecting him as my mother had asked, he turned on me. The pain cut through my chest deep. I felt betrayed and was beyond disappointed. He was so irate; he punched the glass out of the building door and dented my apartment door when he tried to kick it in before storming off. Finally, my uncle and cousin came over and helped resolve the situation. And by the time my brother returned, his clothes were waiting for him on the curb. But trails of blood from his hand smeared the halls. That day I cried. I cried like I had cried at my aunt Mira's funeral. It felt like I had just lost someone to death all over again. I just wanted to escape the pain. But I was much stronger at that point because I had my daughter who kept me focused and gave me strength.

EYE-OPENER

God has a way of opening our eyes to make us focus solely on HIM, to take a seat and rest to prevent becoming burned out. Even HE rested. Although I am obsessed with achieving goals and mastering my challenges, enough is enough after a while. We tend to miss that message but HE will quickly remind us.

Back to school was nearing and the busy season at work was soon to begin. That year by far would be the busiest because we had a site visit to plan for on top of it being recruitment season. In an effort to create balance in my life to keep sane, my summer activities and weekly fun balanced the highly intense fall and winter obligations, allowing me to focus on the prize.
In preparation for the season, I usually hit one of the malls to get the winter shopping done at one time. Star hates to shop so I scooped up my home girl, Tierra, for a day of shopping. Time flew and before we knew it, the stores were closing. The day was fun and I got everything we needed. I dropped Tierra off and right after, got into a car accident.

One of my fears is dying a slow death due to entrapment. I always say a prayer when I drive past an accident on the highway that all survived and have a speedy recovery. On this night, I stopped at a red light at a busy intersection. A traffic agent motioned for me to drive through the red light. I had an uncomfortable feeling in my stomach, as if to question whether she really had things under control despite being the law. But I obeyed her command and eased into the intersection. Before I knew it, another car had shot in front of me from the other direction and I slammed into the side of the car.

Everything seemed to slow and then faded out. I was wide-awake but in a daze. I looked to my left and saw police officers walking toward my car. I got scared and locked my windows and doors. I thought they were coming to harm me or blame me, and at that very moment I was alone and didn't have the words to defend myself. I just looked in the other direction away from them. Then something else happened. A quick flash when I was helpless as a kid.

My stronger and weaker selves were going at it inside my head, and the weaker side was winning. Then my stronger self said, "Get your sh*t together. Shake those emotions off. You have to take care of and defend yourself. If you don't, who will?" I quickly snapped out of my trance and heard a cop asking if I was OK and if I wanted to get out of my car to look at the damage. He had my bent license plates in his hand. I had to be strong and show face; fear had enveloped me and my nerves were shot. I just wanted it to be over so I could go home where it was safe.

I completed the police report, went home, buried my head under my pillow and fell fast asleep.

The next morning, I was supposed to pick up my daughter from her father's house, where she had spent the night, and have a day out in the park for Labor Day, but I didn't have the energy or desire to get out of the bed. My grandmother came over as she usually does to check on me. She was sober and in the mood I needed her to be. When I finally got out of bed, I felt intense pain from head to toe. I was achy. My grandmother insisted that I go to the hospital. I figured that this too would pass and I really just wanted to stay in the bed. Things that are most tragic seem to always be haunting and will forever be mentioned in the future. This would be another topic that I would have to talk about. But I finally agreed to pull myself together to go to the hospital. I got some medication for the pain and returned home.

This accident happened at the very worst time. I was very thankful that I only suffered minor injuries, as things could've been much worse. However, September 1 marked the start of my busy season at work. After the accident, I took a couple of days off with hope that my pains would subside. But I emotionally broke down four days after the accident. I was frustrated and wasn't myself. My daughter was starting school and getting her there and to work was a challenge because of my daily pains. Things really started to weigh on my shoulders. I was falling apart and didn't know where to turn.

I started attending physical therapy but remained overwhelmed between the demands of work and the need to attend my appointments in order to get better. Test results showed that the pain in my foot was from chipped bones in my toe. I thought if I just paid it no attention, the problem would go away on its own.

Time went by. I had already paid for a trip to Miami, but ended up spending most of the time sitting down because I was in pain and had no real energy to engage in many activities. It was such a waste and I started to realize how much this accident had affected me mentally and emotionally. When I got back, I scheduled a visit to the orthopedic surgeon. I was given a boot to begin wearing immediately until I healed. Through this experience, I learned to better take care of myself and to take medication for pain if needed. Not taking care of myself had put me under great physical stress, as well as emotional distress, which even showed up in my performance at my job. My administrator helped me to see the error of my thinking, as well. My job was important, but my priorities had been all wrong. I had more than enough sick time to use to recuperate from my injuries, and I decided to take time needed to fully heal.

I returned to the doctor's for X-rays, which indicated there had been no progress in healing. At that point, I realized I truly needed to sit down.
Over the next month, I had doctor appointments every day, and I was glad that I had taken time off from work.
Once the boot finally came off, I still had to wean myself off the cane and strengthen my leg muscles. Me, who had never been one to rely on anything or anyone. But I believe this experience was designed to happen as it did. Up until that point, my life had been all about surviving. I learned to better prioritize things in my life. If I'm not well, I can't take care of my daughter. Me first then everyone else will fall in line accordingly.

It was the holiday season, which is usually my favorite time of the year but it was rough getting into the spirit.

But just days before Christmas that year, I attended my daughter's end-of-year holiday extravaganza at school and, as it usually did, it got me into the holiday spirit. Better late than never.

However, when Christmas arrived, it was so dreary and I was gloomy all over again. I pulled myself out of the bed to take pictures of Star opening her gifts and climbed right back into my bed.

My brother had welcomed a baby boy the day after my car accident, and he frequently came over with his son to spend time with us. Having the baby around lifted my spirit. He's the cutest little blue-eyed, light-skinned mini me. But sometimes things would get so tense between my brother and the baby's mother that I finally reached a point of not having them over. I hate drama, especially when it is in my comfort zone. I didn't have control for the many years I was forced to witness it as a child, but now I have control and I have zero tolerance for it. When my grandma frequently came over drunk, I would just ignore the door.

One day my cousin Chastity came over to check on me. I love her so. We shared so much over the years and I have learned that the areas where I am stronger she is weaker, and where I am weaker she is stronger. They say opposites attract and our relationship is the perfect example. She has helped me in more ways than even she knows: encouraging me to take risks, love freely and to know that through patience all can happen. During her visit, it felt good to speak about future plans as I usually just lived my days thanking God for seeing another day and hoping to be around to see my great-grandchildren, but never really thinking of future goals and interest.

She was scheduled to get on the highway in a couple of days to take a risk of relocating to pursue her goal of going back to school for her desired degree. This inspired me to step out into a world of the unknown and enjoy the ride while on the journey.

I remember a message being sent to me that read:
The purpose of life is to live it, to taste experience to the utmost, to reach out eagerly and without fear for newer and richer experience. -Eleanor Roosevelt

I was discussing how I intend to take more risks and step outside of my comfort zone in hopes of getting different results.

While we were talking, my door bell rung. My cousin got up to open the door. I then heard the voice of a slurred drunk person and a cloud of darkness fogged my room. My world quickly went from light to dark in an instant. My cousin rarely saw her aunt, my grandmother, in that state. She had only heard stories. My grandma was being obnoxious and saying things that just made me angry. She starting spilling beer on my floor, and I lost my cool because I hate when my mop smells like anything other than housecleaning supplies. I told her to leave. I hopped out of the bed and in all my anger, totally forgot to put the boot on and had to focus on not applying pressure on the foot. In my trying to get past her to get my mop, my grandmother pushed her weight on the knee and tried to step on my wounded foot and make me fall. For a second, my grandmother was my enemy. I went to grab for her neck before my cousin jumped in between us. I cursed her out like I never did before. I was so fed up and at the point where I was at my lowest, I expected different. I broke down and just cried. My cousin did what she does best, consoled me, but then gave me the words of encouragement needed to decrease the energy wasted on the negative feelings I had. Being kicked while I was down was my eye opener.

Not long after that incident, I had another experience on New Year's Eve, this time with my brother and his girlfriend. I was out of the boot and moving around the best I could. I decided to cook and have my brother and his family over. My brother had been drinking before he got to my house and that was the start of a disastrous evening. The food was ready to be eaten when all arrived and in less than two hours the ball would be dropping. Before dinner, we went around the table to speak of what we were thankful. The responses from him and his girlfriend turned me off for the evening and I decided to end the party early. But all agreed to be on their best behavior until the ball dropped within minutes. However, once the ball dropped, I was on the phone calling a cab just as all hell had broken loose and my brother and his girlfriend were going at it strong, causing a huge scene.

My brother and my grandma, the two people in whom I have invested the most, have caused me the highest levels of stress and depression. Yet before now, I had never understood how to turn off that switch. There was a great sense of obligation there. My mother's last words to take care of them rang in my head constantly. It's as if I was being reminded for a different reason. A reminder to stop. I knew better and had heard it for years, but I had to get to that place of understanding on my own. It is now fully understood and the pain felt is a reminder of what not to do.
I bumped up on the message below to describe my mood during those dreadful times. We often know the truth, but it can help to see it written. It was so fitting:

- I am tired of crying.
- I am tired of yelling.
- I am tired of being sad.
- I am tired of pretending.
- I am tired of being alone.
- I am tired of feeling crazy.
- I am tired of feeling stuck.
- I am tired of needing help.
- I am tired of remembering.
- I am tired of missing things.
- I am tired of being different.
- I am tired of missing people.
- I am tired of feeling worthless.
- I am tired of feeling empty inside.
- I am tired of not being able to just let go.
- I am tired of wishing I could start all over.
- I am tired of dreaming of a life I will never have.
- But most of all, I am just tired of being tired. - *Unknown*

I was now out of the boot and preparing to go back to work to get back into the swing of living my life again. I gained a different appreciation of life even more than before.

Despite returning to work, there were still some residual issues. The frequency and intensity of headaches had increased since the accident, and I scheduled visits to see a neurologist and psychologist. My first encounter with the clinical psychologist was brief, but during subsequent visits, I completed a survey, described the accident and then did a series of tests that I found mentally exhausting. One was a Rorschach exam during which I was shown ink blots with pictures and asked to describe what I saw. I performed various connect-the-dots tasks that were timed. Then there was a word phrase I had to define using symbols given and also under time constraints. Last, but not least, was a test of my memory. Remembering a series of numbers read forward and backward. I gave up after recalling a series of about six to seven digits. It felt like my head was about to explode. During my next visit, I would get results and I was very curious.

I grew more and more anxious as my appointment date to receive my results neared, but to my surprise, doctors found my intellectual level to be pretty high. That overshadowed his next set of findings from the exams: controlling, angry, high levels of anxiety, traumatized and depressed. The sound of these words ringing in the air had me, in my mind, shouting, crying, screaming, rolling around on the floor, clapping and snapping, but outwardly, I was calm. Everything I know to be true and he found me out through exams. The doctor asked me about my dreams and asked that I start keeping a journal. The thought of chronicling the dreams that had haunted me for years—and him being able to give me the remedy to take them away.

I kept a dream diary, and during my next meeting, we discussed my entries. From the characters and nature of the dreams, the clinician discerned that I was running from something or someone in the South. I was overwhelmed with joy and relieved that someone knew me without me having to say much about me. Someone who knew me better than me. But the experience was also unsettling. After the session, I was embarrassed and felt naked. I was referred to the psychologist. There was much more to be learned about myself and I had high hopes of healing.

As I was leaving the room when the appointment ended, the doctor said, "Diamond, you should do something with your intellects."

This was the second time hearing that within a couple weeks of each other. I had recently taken my daughter to see her dermatologist. After three visits and conversing with the doctor, he asked what I did for living and does it involve teaching. Once I told him what I do and it happen to be in an education sector, he then said Diamond, you should go back to school for your masters. You will do well. Puzzled because he had no knowledge of what level of schooling I had. Nonetheless that was a sign to pursue the goals of going back to school that has been on hold until I got the sudden urge to do so.

Over the years, I have had many therapy sessions, none of which I found helpful. I was always left more frustrated. I expected someone to help me make sense of all that had happened and to take my pain away. I wanted my mom back, my heart pain to go away, the memory to be erased and life to be as I remembered it before the tragedy. In my earlier sessions, directly following my mother's death, I said and shared nothing. To try to get through to me, doctors would ask me to draw pictures of what was on my mind. I was lost and disinterested. However, in later years, when I realized I needed help, my approach was different. I never had a problem sharing what was on my heart and mind. I just simply wanted to leave a therapy session feeling relieved. Instead my anger grew.

REVISITING

In 2009, I reconnected with my family and childhood family and classmates before the tragedy. Anastasia was the cousin from my Grandpa Beaken's side of the family with whom I used to play often. My mother had had a great relationship with her father, and we were very close to his side of the family. Right before the gas mask was placed on my face during surgery to repair my injuries following the attack, I had asked if I would ever see Anastasia again. But while I could remember that moment like it was yesterday, I could not remember the times I had shared with Anastasia or with anyone before everything happened.

She reached out to me on Facebook. To confirm my identity, she asked questions about my mother and knew the year everything took place. Tears welled up in my eyes. Jacob and his sister Melanie, my classmates and best friends from grade school, contacted me next. Jacob was my grade school crush and it was interesting to hear the stories that he remembered about my mom and me. But after a while, it became overwhelming and frustrating as there was much I didn't remember that was enjoyable and the things I did remember were painful.

So I decided to go back to South Carolina to visit everyone. My relocation to New York had been for my own protection in many ways. However, I felt like I had run all my life and that facing the past wasn't necessary. It almost seemed as if running was always the best thing to do, as that's what happened when Mommy passed away. We fled the South with no exchanged connections.

Reflecting back, at 13, I went back to Orangeburg to spend time with my friend Tara and her mom. They had moved from their previous location, which had been right across the street from where everything took place. Tara's grandmother still lived there and wanted to see me. So we took a route that would allow me to avoid anyone seeing me.

The visit started out great. We sat around playing catch-up while dinner was cooking. Then there was a knock on the door. It was

Tara's friend, the niece of the monster. She was a few years older than us. She smiled and said hello. There was a brief moment when she and I were alone, and she took the time to remind me that her uncle was coming back to get me. That he said he was going to finish what he started. That everyone thought I hadn't made it, and that she would be sure to tell him I did.

I was so scared I took off running to see if my uncle or great-grandmother was at home. I ran out the back door, and through the backyard that led to my old house where everything had taken place and where my grandmother's brother Uncle Ben was now living. He was sitting on the porch. Running as fast as I could, out of breath and with a face full of tears, I explained to my uncle what had happened. He was drunk, but stumbled in to get his shotgun. To my shock, a car drove by and the face of the monster was eyeing us and laughing. I later found out it the man in the car was the monster's father. Terrified, I just hid behind my uncle crying, with my eyes closed tightly and hands over my ears as he aimed the shotgun at the car. After what seemed like forever, I opened my eyes and he hugged me and told me everything was going to be fine and that no one was going to hurt me again.

In planning my visit as an adult to go see my childhood family and friends in South Carolina, I wanted to make sure the monster was still incarcerated, so I searched on the state website for inmates with hopes that I could confirm the release date of my mother's killer. The relatives who were supposed to be contacted—my uncle Bob and aunts Mira and Deidre —had all passed away. I was scanning through the site and every face that popped up brought more fear and a feeling that salt was being sprinkled over my wounds. I closed the site before I found what I had set out to find. A couple of days later, my reoccurring nightmares started again, which brought on a panic attack. I was in McDonald's eating and my mind began playing tricks on me. Someone walked in with the face of the man I remembered to have hurt me. I froze. He stared at me and I returned the stare. He sat right behind me. In all my nervousness, I gathered my things but when I tried to get up to move my knees were locked. I had to massage them and calm my nerves before making a dash for it. At that moment, I realized I was not ready to make that visit. Instead, I sought help.

My first few visits with the psychologist I referred to by the clinician after the car accident were very different from what I had previously experienced. She set a different tone. "This is a relationship," she said. "If you give me some, I can give you some, but if you only give me a little, that will not be enough to give you any." To have never been in a give-and-take relationship or to have a sense of hope that the light and greatness at the end of the tunnel was closer than I knew, intrigued me.

In discussing the accident, the conversation went to places much further back in time until the rug was pulled and all that I had swept under it was now fully revealed. It was like that storage shed, basement or closet that is rarely visited. There can be so much junk in that dark, cold, cobweb-filled space.

Overtime, the therapist and I slowly sorted through and began to discard items that had been outgrown. There were other items that were put aside to look over again because through those I realized where my flaws and feelings derived from. It now made sense and was allowing me to accept the things I can't change about me. Finally, there were items I was slow to approach and hesitant to touch. There were insects surrounding them. All my fears were uncovered. Knocking the insects away, one by one, I have carefully taken a look at each one of them.

"How did I overcome when the weight of the world was heavy on my shoulders?" I asked. If I believe that God has brought me past these situations, the residue of remembrance can reside in storage. But staring fear in the face, realizing the power and control it has had over me, and still allowing it to continue to take up space in my head contradicts my beliefs. HE has protected me through the impossible, provided me with strength when I was weary, and guidance when I was lost. Fear was immediately discarded. I have grown to learn that I had the power and answers all along. First acknowledging and accepting was the key. I was too weak to revisit and travel down memory lane, but am learning that revisiting has brought about much strength, strength to finally live with no constraints.

Without this revisit and better understanding of who I am, appreciating me may have never happened.

****

When she was 8, my daughter came to me and asked, "Mommy, when did your mom die? I responded, "When I was 9 years old." She asked the month and day, and then hugged me, saying, "Mommy, I don't want you to die."

It touched me because I had had the same fear for years. I had to soothe her and tell her that I wasn't going anywhere and hopefully for a longtime. She is blessed to have seven grandparents and great-grandparents combined. So long life is possible. In the meantime, we are going to create everlasting memories and make a mark that can be remembered in this lifetime. Every day I feed her knowledge and teach her survival tactics, just in case. When I was her age, there was much I didn't know how to do. But my daughter has been tying her shoes since age 3, braiding her dolls' hair since she was 5, ironing since the age of 7 and able to use the microwave and toaster to warm her food.

In this healing process, there are parts of me that are still under construction. I have lived my life too scared to get into a relationship or close to people for fear of losing them or that they may hurt me. So to protect myself, I deal with people from a distance. Those who managed to get past my boundaries usually did so because our spirits somehow connected and the internal green light was granted, forcing the gates down.

One of the things I pray for is that I never witness any more tragedies. The sounds of fighting or someone suffering or deteriorating, either in real life or in a movie, are traumatizing to me. Watching my aunts Mira and Margaret deteriorate from healthy, strong woman to frail and weak souls down to their last days tore me up inside, making it so hard to concentrate during my day to day. It was frightening and traumatizing. I recently saw the movie

Best Man 2; to see Mia sick and going through the motions had me in uncontrollable tears. I felt like walking out, but in an effort to heal myself, I sat through it and prayed.

A friend sent me the following message. I printed it and placed in my apartment. I tried to apply these points in hopes of becoming a better me:

Last week I threw out WORRY, it was getting old and in the way.
It kept me from being me; I could not do things God's way.
I threw out a book on MY PAST (Didn't have time to read it anyway).
Replaced it with NEW GOALS and started reading it today.
I threw out HATE and BAD MEMORIES. (Remember how I treasured them so)
Got me a NEW PHILOSOPHY too and threw out the one from long ago.
Brought in some new books too called I CAN, I WILL, and I MUST.
Threw out I MIGHT, I THINK and I OUGHT. WOW, you should've seen the dust!
I ran across an OLD FRIEND, I had not talked to in a while.
His name is GOD my FATHER, and I really like HIS style.
He helped me to do some cleaning and added some things HIMSELF.
Like PRAYER, HOPE, FAITH and LOVE.
Yes, I placed them right on the shelf.
I picked up this special thing and placed it at the front door.
I FOUND IT - it's called PEACE. Nothing gets me down anymore.
-Unknown

All of the points mentioned seem very simple to incorporate into your daily living. Easier said than done. HE is my protective shield and has our back and best interest at heart. If we the people can just get past our fears, insecurities and worries and gear the freed energy into something constructive to better ourselves, life will have greater meaning and value.

After having taken a seven-year break, I decided to go back to school to pursue a master's degree in psychology. I not only hoped to gain a better understanding of myself, I wanted to assist in creating a platform that gives hope to individuals in need; to be a voice that is heard and to be one that is able to share an uplifting word based on my experiences.

There is something about listening, speaking to and sharing information with someone when his or her experiences are relatable. Pain is pain, just as sin is sin, and isn’t weighed on a scale. Paper cuts hurt too, and at times, hurt more than deeper cuts. We will all at some point in life be able to relate to another's pain as we will all go through it, just at different times in life.

SELF-ASSESSMENT—WHO AM I?

Finding happiness and for all to be well with my soul, to be healed, so I can fully begin to live life, was always my focus and fantasy.

Before my daughter became ill with Stevens-Johnson, I used to be depressed daily, more hours than not. Every so often, I would get a weird feeling of excitement for about a couple of seconds. The feeling would quickly go away, but it felt so good, I was on a mission to feel that feeling often. Right after my daughter spoke to me in the hospital after she had been unconscious for so many days, that good feeling filled me almost immediately, and rarely today do I feel depressed more than a few seconds a day. I learned that the things we focus our attention on might not be something on which to define our happiness in life. It's the simple things that we should hang on to for continuous happiness, such as breathing and life.

"Speak in such a way that others love to listen to you. Listen in such a way that others love to speak to you." - Unknown

The gift I have been blessed with is my personality. Everyone tends to gravitate to a warm, free-spirited, genuine soul. Genuine and positive energy runs through my veins from the depth of my soul. It wasn't always that way, but after realizing, accepting and appreciating self and that I'm where I'm supposed to be in life, it became pretty easy to free myself of all the unfulfilled feelings that consumed me.

I have a huge group of friends, associates and family that entrust me with their most intimate secrets or just to be that rational ear. I have never passed judgment or, better yet, used the things that I knew of someone else to boost my own feelings about myself. Looking back on it, relating someone else's issues to my own life may have helped open my eyes to see that I'm not the only one in the struggle. I used to feel that no one else's issues were comparable. But while the issues may be different, as we have different walks in life, we all have hang-ups and a mound of issues we are battling.

I am to the people in my life, what I hope for. ♦

In being a listener and shoulder to many, there were times I also offered my opinions. In most instances, most just wanted to vent without criticism or interjections. I have learned that it is very important to share and communicate your issues and problems, especially with people who can fully relate and are interested in you as their friend. People who will be an ear or give you more than a "You'll be fine." or "You'll get through it like you got through the other situations." Although this is the truth, there are times when you want to know that you aren't the only one going through something.

I have the ability to genuinely empathize with another. I allow myself to enter a person's mind and heart when he or she tells his or her issues and can share relatable stories for comfort. I know this because I become emotionally depleted afterwards, and even when the person is long gone, the thoughts still live with me as if the person's experiences were my own.

I am also a thinker. Some people see it as overanalyzing. In more ways than one, being a thinker has helped me during this journey.

Life is about the decisions you make. I have always made decisions after thinking of all the possible options and outcomes, along with what feels right. I recall feeling as if I may not have made the best decisions at times because I ended up at square one or having to start again. At times, there are no right or wrong answers to situations we are faced with. I would get to a fork in the road and become conflicted about which way is best. Going right maybe bumpier, going straight may have a dead end and going left may be a curvier path with many steep hills.

I have been forced for more years of my life than most, to make decisions. Most of my challenges in life have been faced alone. I believe people mean well and their opinions and advice are respected and appreciated. However, if that advice doesn't come from an experienced place, it holds very little weight to me.

Most of my feedback and advice comes from my life experiences.

I rarely get into my feelings, but I do realize my levels of anger and anxiety are super high and they don't work well together. It has gotten so much better since I have begun to assess and accept who I am.

At times I feel high-strung. Like pot on boil. I can read an email or text and depending on my mood, take their message the wrong way. Because I am aware of this, I often take a moment and then revisit the text when I have calmed myself. I like to call it a five-step process of calming. I first, close my eyes, breathe, then tell myself it is not as it seems or is not that serious, close it out and finally plan to revisit when I can see clearer.

When I was much younger, after the tragedy, I would bite my nails down to the meat, sometimes to the point that they bled. I didn't even realize when I stopped because by then I had moved on to something else extreme to keep my mind focused.
So from intense work projects to listening to music that soothes me, it is imperative that I have music in my day to day, engaging in daily activities that relax me is necessary.

I have high expectations for myself in any and everything I do. I am easily disappointed with myself if my daily "To Do" lists aren't close to being done or completed in a day.

Sadly, I leave no space for error or unforeseen issues.

I constantly fill my schedule to avoid thinking of or being in that dark place I have grown to hate. I am fearful of being in that state again. It's mentally overwhelming and physically draining.

I have changed to give more, if not all, of my attention to self so that I can see me as most others see me. Better yet, how God sees me. My therapist explained that I give freely to people in need as it gives the satisfaction I didn't get by not being able to save my mother. And at one point in my life, it made me happy to make another happy. But I have come to realize that some of the "take-take" relationships I've been in have been due to this nature.

Staying focused and keeping my mind and eyes on the prize keep me sane. Creating realistic, short-term daily, weekly and monthly goals helps to keep me well balanced and confident in knowing that I am that much closer to achieving my goals. Succeeding.

Facing challenges has been a way of life and how I survived. Life has never gotten easier. I have just grown stronger and have gained a better understanding of what to expect. Acceptance has played a huge role.

CHANGE

Why is there such a thing as day and night?

Why is it important to have different seasons?

Why do we age?

These are all natural occurrences that are part of life. Change is not always good, but it takes us out of our comfort zone. It's necessary for our survival. If things stayed the same, we wouldn't grow and life wouldn't be as interesting.

Change is needed to break a dollar bill.

Change was always disturbing to me. As early as I could remember, my primary focus was on trying to find a routine and master it to make life that much easier for me. Transitions and adjustments were forced on me too early in life. However, despite the results being different when change was introduced, it was the act of learning to adjust to the unknown that proved useful.

I conditioned myself to get into the habit of breaking habits so that when change happened, I could be mentally prepared.

I approached every situation tactfully, with a thought-out plan. Over the years, I have gotten better with accepting change. Change will happen even if I'm not prepared.

In the workplace, change will take place even if I'm not onboard for it. Knowing that, I have grown to accept change in those areas where I have no choice. Much of my life revolved around work, to provide for my family, and my education because school kept me focused. I always had to work to survive, while school was an option and an outlet.

However, it took some time to apply the acceptance of change to my personal life where there was much more flexibility.
Changing the people that meant a lot to me, but took more from me

than they gave, was difficult to notice and accept.

Working to change my need to want what I didn't have during my youth from the ones I thought I should have gotten it from is still a work in progress. I have forgiven and finally accepted my grandmother for who she is because she did the very best she knew how with the lack thereof in her own experiences during her own childhood. The guilt and pain led to her alcohol and drug abuse, which changed and got the very best of the person I knew. Like me, many people can attest that she is a wonderful person with a beautiful spirit and heart when she is sober. Very loved and respected, she is the reason for my strength. Although many painful moments live within me, the experience pushed me to all limits and made me the strong individual I am today. Despite it all, there is nothing I wouldn't do for her.

Change must happen to grow and this is what we hope will continue as we age.

WHAT'S CONSIDERED NORMAL WHEN WE ARE ALL UNIQUE?

We are all uniquely different. My eyes being green and changing with the colors I wear, and my sandy brown hair make me different from many. Some may even consider the differences to be deformities.

Is it normal to feel that the things within ourselves with which we are not content, are not normal?

For years, I had identity issues. I couldn't see any physical features that were similar to those of my mom or my dad. And it was hard embracing my differences and appreciating them as their being the makeup God wanted me to have. Being called a white girl with nappy hair, or recognized for having tiny lips and no ear lobes was hurtful; it added to the awkward feelings I had. Oddly enough those comments always came from my own people, which contributed to my feelings of not belonging. Interestingly, I have always been easily accepted in any other races.

Today, I am appreciative of the cloth from which I am cut, which makes me love me better and understand the reasons for my views and why I move the way I do in life.

We all have our own perceptions as to what is normal. To not have my immediate family's love, affection and support wasn't normal to me growing up. Getting what I needed from others all those years was and is much appreciated. However, none of it changed the want for my mother and aunt who had moved on to a better place, leaving me here to fend for myself on Earth. Then, having all that topped off with a cherry and whipped cream by my father rejecting me and later disowning me.

Friends have said how lucky I am to have succeeded in all I set out to achieve. Sadly, I don't feel as lucky as I should and am often jealous of what they have, such as their moms and family structures. If I could trade all that I have gained and achieved to have all that I lost, I would.

With confidence and a better understanding today, the following is no longer a factor, but I spent most of my life internalizing and criticizing many things about myself. People who seemed to only know how to criticize surrounded me.

Many are quick to judge, but we are all similarly broken.

For example, when I read the book *Fifty Shades of Grey* by E.L. James, I was intrigued. Not for the obvious reason of the sex acts the book details, but because of the reasons behind the main character's abnormal characteristics being displayed in someone so overtly successful. Mr. Grey's being fifty shades of f*cked up due to childhood experiences, is normal, yet sick, to most people who can't relate. Things we are traumatized by often become acts we commit to find satisfaction. Thus, what is normal to you, others may frown upon.

Mr. Grey's feeling about wasting food because he had experienced starvation as a child was another behavior that caught my attention. Similarly, in my youth, there were many nights I starved. Now, I make it a point to eat all that I put on my plate, even if I feel I'm about to pop, and I insist on my daughter eating all that is on her plate to avoid waste. I find that I always make mention of the many starving people in the world.

Making it to the checkout line in the supermarket and not having enough money and then having to put food back were normal and embarrassing for me as a child. Now, I go in the supermarket without a budget and rarely a list. I now know why it's so satisfying to me; I am making up for all that I didn't have when I had no control. The subconscious mind is amazing. I also like things in abundance just to have an option. There were no choices growing up. It excites me to see a variety of cereal choices on the top of my fridge or in the cabinet, or having many different fragrances of body sprays, perfumes and lotions. This may sound crazy, but during my youth, there were times we ran out of soap and toilet paper and had to use newspaper to wipe after defecating, and even later finding out while washing the family laundry, that members of my family were also using their clothes. I remember it like it was yesterday. I was responsible for washing everyone in the household's clothes. One day, when I was sorting clothes to put in to wash, my hand got stuck in something slimy. When I looked at my hand, there was human sh*t on it and it smelled terribly. I was so pissed and just made it a point to make sure that there wouldn't be a need for this to happen in my future. So, buying toilet tissue and soaps in bulk is a must.

What Mr. Grey witnessed as a child became a part of him as he grew. He displayed avoidant attachment, aggressive and possessive behaviors. Kinky sex leading to punishments and abuse was what fulfilled his fantasy. Having a separate room for the women he was intimate with to sleep because they weren't allowed to sleep in his bed was sick, weird and twisted. But I totally related.

Having been molested by my aunt and touched and fondled by a boy and a man made me a sexual person, but uncomfortable in close proximity to women. This has changed over the years as comfort was needed and I became big on hugs. When I gained mental control, and knew that no one could violate me again because I could protect myself, I allowed that dormant part of me to flourish and just be. But it was a process reconditioning myself. Before this, when a hug was warranted, the moment our bodies got too close, I found myself counting to five, releasing my grip and pulling back first. It got weird when I pulled back but the other person still had me in a tight grip. When hugging a male, I would hug him while keeping a lot of space between our private areas by sticking my butt back.

Having watched a man brutally hurt me and my mom, and seeing other close relatives give women serious beatdowns, caused me to have an emotional disconnect when dealing with men and on defense. I have no tolerance for aggressive, insecure behaviors. These have been signs that I've experienced when dealing with men, which I have picked up on, and lo' and behold, the truth of having abusive behaviors has revealed itself inevitably.

I could have a casual sexual moment and walk away as if it never happened. Using my powers and control to make up for the powerless feeling I had when I couldn't defend myself, I considered sex recreation, an activity with very little meaning to me. It was a light switch that I could easily turn on and off. I went on many sabbaticals when focused. Then there were those times when I became a beast and needed it. Unless I had developed feelings and we were in a relationship or there were talks of one in the near future, there was no connection between my pleasure buttons and emotions. It had always been easiest to control situations with fewer feelings because disappointment didn't exist.

My sexual feelings were heavily influenced by the amount of alcohol in my system. My alter ego was at her best, in full swing, when the alcohol was in my system. In the past, when I was severely depressed, I drank to get drunk. I became less worried and stressed, and felt in charge and in better control of myself. I had such a great feeling of freedom; freedom from the constant, reoccurring memories of my past that had parked and set up shop in my head. However, the behaviors and activities that took place often left me disappointed, with regret and horrible hangovers.

I now only drink at social events, or maybe have a glass of wine at home. I have decreased my alcohol intake to a two-drink maximum, and it works much better and leaves none of the negative residue.

To me, it is quite normal to change faces to fit the scene. I handle my business to the best of my ability and my reward is taking myself to a temporary place where all my needs and wants exist and are met.

Judging someone has never been a part of my character simply because I don't like being judged. No one truly understands you better than you.

Judging this book by its cover, will shock most who have known me for years and never knew my story. It may even change your thoughts about me, based on your previous perception.

RELATIONSHIPS

Disappointment, rejection, love and loss of individuals will happen at some point in our lives.

Having expectations caused the greatest feeling of disappointment. Expecting that a person who claimed to be my friend had my best interests at heart, or that a boss I looked up to highly due to his or her role, education, experience, or position would respect subordinates or provide mentorship, was quite disappointing.

I have learned that there are few mentors and many people are just plain selfish. It's as if we are all crabs in a barrel fighting to survive. Extending myself to help another gives me great pleasure but I am realizing doing so is not within us all.
I strive to have like people in my circle, positive, driven, honest, loving and respectful people. When it comes to relationships, these factors play a huge role for me. The success of something long-term seems to be impossible with the many hang-ups I have.

Therapy is allowing me to see the error and reasoning in my ways and the thinking that's been brought about from my tragedies, losses and abuse. Through some very effective therapy sessions, I am that much closer to releasing myself from the shackles and breaking down the walls that surround me.

Mother

Abandonment and rejection are two of the worst issues that affect me today. My mom's leaving me was out of her control, but my heart and mind at the age it happened couldn't understand that, and my dad's taking a walk at the same time was hurtful and continued to affect me because of his inconsistency and giving false hope.

There is no love like a mother's love. I remember being at my uncle Steve's 50th birthday party, taking in the crowd. Everyone was getting down. I imagined my mother and Aunt Mira being there, living and enjoying the fun, doing a two-step to prove that they still had it. Tears welled in my eyes from the thought. I felt so alone at that moment.

I missed out on the mother-daughter relationship. Admiring the young lady who had taken on a household to care for her sibling and young children, I wonder would we have been close, or too much alike, causing us to clash? Would she have been in the front row at my graduations, fashion shows, music and dance recitals screaming my name as loud as she could because she was so proud of me? Would she have been my travel buddy with people mistaking us for sisters because of how young she would look next to me? When I was pregnant, what words of advice would she have given me? Considering her dislike for New York, would we have ever made a visit to the Big Apple? Most of all, would she have been there to pick me up when I fell and tell me, "It is OK, dust yourself off and try again"? There are many questions to which I would never have the answers.

My mother struggled in her lifetime, but the act of doing so showed strength and courage. She lived and fought a hard battle that may have been endless with limited resources if she had survived. I often feel that Mommy would've wanted to live to take care of us after the attack. But looking at the war scars all over her body may have had its effects on her. I often sit and wonder how she would've lived with herself if I hadn't made it and perhaps feeling as if she didn't do enough to save me. I wonder because I live with the feeling that I didn't do enough to save her. I had major issues over the years looking at and showing my own scars. However, I got to a point of looking at the situation differently. I once only wore one-piece bathing suits, now two-piece bathing suits are all I wear. Every so often, someone will ask if I had a caesarean. It catches me off-guard sometimes because I forget the scars are there. Now I appreciate my scars because they represent only a memory of my mother and our last moments we shared.

Her memory is indeed etched in stone. God blessed her with a gift to be able to share her life story and give another hope. The year I graduated college, I realized that I was the same age my mom was the day she was scheduled to graduate and everything happened. It was a pretty spooky feeling. Then there was the time I was planning Star's first birthday party. I was down in the dumps. I felt so alone. I wished that my mother and aunt were there to share in these moments of my life. How could You have taken the two closest people away from me? I said a prayer before bed that night, and to my surprise my mother paid me a visit. I remember her asking me, "Why are you so down?" Not waiting for my response, she just simply said, "Introduce me to my granddaughter. Cheer up, and show me the themes you purchased already for her party." We walked and talked slowly over a bridge. There was beautiful blue and green water under it. Amazingly, when I woke up, the night before's feelings didn't exist.

She, alongside God, has been my strength, my eyes when I can't see, the wind beneath my wings, the air I breathe.

It's only when I allowed myself to accept GOD in my life did things become clearer. It's only when we accept things for what they are do we begin to live and get what God and life have to offer. Not doing so was my own hindrance. When we know better, we do better. She will be forever missed and live in my heart.

Father

I knew my father but he wasn't consistently in my life. In fact, as an adult with a child I realized he was never fit for or capable of fatherhood and being around us. Whenever he did come around, maybe once a month, his presence always did bring joy because for children, the absentee parent tends to be more appealing and appreciated at the moment. His leaving always left a negative taste in my and my brother's mouths.

We really didn't see him as frequently after he returned my brother to my mom with white powder under his nose. It seemed like we moved around a lot to avoid him. My mother had also finally moved on from him. But although he knew he couldn't do right, my father still managed to come around and make matters worse. He wasn't capable of being a man, or a father. God removed people from our lives for a reason. I'm not certain of the person I would've become or the characteristics and qualities I would've possessed had he been the one to raise my brother and me. Wanting love and attention from my dad, would've cost me a world of other issues. I'm thanking my higher being for a better understanding today.

Children love their parents unconditionally. With this in mind, we love them endlessly and continue to strive to please and impress them for greater love.

My father has always disappointed me. He gave us money for Picture Day one night and before we woke up the next morning, he had taken the money back, leaving and promising to come see us but never making doing so. After the tragedy, when we searched my hospital drawer and realized he had stolen the money I needed to pay for TV and phone services while I was recovering, he again left, saying he was too busy to spend the night with me, leaving me feeling violated and rejected.

On my 21st birthday, I received a message on my answering machine from him. With everything happening during those dark years of my life, I was overjoyed. He remembered my birthday. By this time, it had been three years since the last time I had seen him when he had stopped the bus my brother and I were on to head home from South Carolina. We were off to a good start. He seemed to be much more consistent in his calling.

Some years later, after giving birth to Star and visiting his mom, Grandma Flore, was the first time we spent time together. He was very protective of his granddaughter Star and shared that I had looked the same as a baby. It was touching; as he held her, swaying and whispering to her, it seemed as if he was reminiscing. I figured he would be a better grandfather than he had been a father. Wrong! At the end of that year, I had convinced him to spend time with us in the big city. I had planned to get my nephew Brice, who had just been born, so that he could meet his new grandson as well. He agreed and I bought him a ticket and awaited his arrival. I was looking forward to family time with him. He walked through my door, got settled, then looked at me and said, "You know I'm not your father right? Your mother cheated on me with a white man." He mentioned the name of the man.

I was taken aback. This was a first. And my mother was no longer around to defend herself. But it explained his behavior toward me—and why I'm a "high yellow" complexion with green eyes and sandy colored hair. When I was a child, my grandmother would tease me and say that they had found me in a big, brown chair in the woods and that I was adopted. My great-great-grandmother and some of her sisters had been very light of complexion, but none had eyes that changed colors. I had always wanted to believe my coloring was in the genes of my ancestors or that I was special, different.

With mixed emotions and a need to protect myself so the man I called father wouldn't see how hurt I was, I simply responded by asking him to repeat the name of the man he had identified as being my biological father. "What is the name again?" I asked. "Maybe I can reach out to him and build the relationship after all these years."

My father had the audacity to snap, "That wasn't nice. How could you say something like that?" I had purchased his one-way ticket and was now so anxious for him to get the hell out at that moment without contributing to his return ticket.

After that, we didn't speak for some years until he called me, stressed out because he had some money and it seemed like he was in some type of danger. He wanted to send me some money to hold or to use if I needed, considering my brother was back in jail and needed a package that he was aware of. I told him no, advising he dig a hole in the back of his yard and bury it until he needed it. He laughed, but I was serious. I reminded him of our last encounter and shared with him how painful it had been. He went back on his word and said he didn't say that. In desperation, he accused me of not hearing what I heard and then told me that I was his daughter.

Some time later, he mailed me $500, which I used to buy items that I boxed up and sent to my brother. A couple of months later, after talking to him about once or twice a week, my aunt called to tell me he was running around telling people I took his money. My uncle called with the same story. When I confronted him, my father denied it. I was sick of his lies. I cursed him out, and told him to never call me again. My uncle called me about a year ago to tell me my father had had a stroke, and as God is my witness, the news didn't move me. I moved on to a new topic.

My father calls every two years. I didn't realize it until recently, but when he calls, he asks how everyone is doing except for me and my baby, Star. So I gave it to him with double barrels again. There's no need to call me on behalf of your son, I told him. Stop wasting your time because it only gets my blood to boiling. My father lacks respect, acknowledgment and consistency. I have grown to realize that what I want from him, I will never get.

Children are parents' investment. If you do right by your kids, your kids will help you when you are in need as they grow into adults and make lives for themselves.

Recently, I told my father how much I hated him for walking out, leaving us to feel rejected and abandoned; for not being what I needed him to be as a parent and causing me to have issues in the relationship department because of his being my role model of what a man was supposed to stand for. His response? That he felt the same way, as if we had abandoned him and didn't care for him. It took everything in me not to curse him out. I needed to have this adult conversation and get as much as I needed out of it. So I simply responded, "You are the parent and we are the kids. You walked out when Mommy died."

He apologized, but I wanted to know if he truly understood what he was apologizing for. I told him how painful it was when he told me I wasn't his daughter because of how different I look. He said he didn't remember saying that but that he was sorry and I was his child. He said he played the blame game all these years because he didn't know any better. He didn't know how to right the wrong. That this was what he knew growing up. He was abandoned, and instead of doing better for his kids, he opted to repeat the cycle.

I felt a great sense of relief. It was like heavy weights were lifted off my shoulders. From that very moment, I felt free. The floodgates of emotions flowed freely like a waterfall. I was sure that he was there to stay and that our relationship would change. Maybe not a daughter and father relationship, exactly, but one where we could start having open conversation about ourselves. Wishful thinking. The change lasted for about a month. Now we are going on year 2 of no communication.

My father failed me, but I am grateful that at least the man who's in my daughter's life has been to her what I yearned for. Both parents are necessary. It is particularly important to have a father in his daughter's life to assist in her upbringing and to build a bond that will help her develop into a more secure, balanced adult.

Though my father had always been many miles away in the South, my brother has his genes and exercises his same behaviors. And with my father's treatment of me and not having him in much of my life, I have been attracted to men like my father, men with similarly negative characteristics and qualities.

Grandma and Brother

My grandmother and my brother have been like children that I have taken care of throughout my life. I have been there when they have fallen on many occasions.

I have been a parent to my brother more than half his life. I missed out on the sibling experience of fighting and making up. Of sharing stories of school life and taking trips together to amusement parks. I was more accustomed to him being my protector, ready to fight anyone who posed a threat. It was pretty hard to tell him no when he was in need, and yes, this has enabled him. He has been in jail most of his teenage and adult life, making it very hard to build the kind of relationship that I wanted. When he is home, I am always optimistic that he will get it together and grow up. He is a good person, but the moment I get used to having a piece of my past near, he ends up right back in jail. A lot of my brother's issues derive from our past as well. A huge sense of guilt consumes him for not making it back in time to save Mommy when he went for help. His need to protect me fills a certain void. It is comforting to him.

I love my grandmother to pieces, and despite all the pain, I am ever so grateful that she made certain sacrifices to care for my brother and me. Life hasn't gotten the best of me yet because of it. As I get older and accept many things, I understand her pain and the reasons she does what she does. She is the strongest woman I know to have lost many and much and still remain standing.
When alcohol is abused, it becomes a disease. You step outside yourself and become someone else. She did the best she could with what she knew.

After the argument we had when I almost hit her when she was trying to inflict pain on my injured foot, she left as I asked and it was over a month before I saw her again. I didn't think about her or concern myself with her. Then, on the Thanksgiving following our argument, I woke up annoyed, but couldn't pinpoint why. After about an hour, I manage to get up and cook and realized that I wished that my grandmother were there to share the food as she usually did every Thanksgiving. About thirty minutes later, my doorbell rung and it was she. I was internally jumping up and down like a kid.
Another time, I had this same feeling after a nightmare that woke me up in a cold sweat. It was around 8:45a.m., and my doorbell rang. It seems I felt her just as it seems she felt me. I hugged her so long and hard. She hugged me, and it just made up for other times when she didn't do it.

It was so weird; the one who inflicted a lot of pain was the person I wanted so bad to comfort me. Something that is often the case in abusive relationships.

My brother, father and grandmother Meena's behavior toward me truly showed how hard they took my mother's death. Me being the spitting image of her was a reminder they couldn't handle. I am aware today, and have a better understanding of how to deal with them, which has allowed me to forgive and accept them as they are.

CLOSER THAN CLOSE RELATIONSHIPS

Relationships with men had always been a challenge. Taking a risk and letting my guard down to truly allow someone to be my rock was difficult.

I tended to gravitate toward abusive situations and stay in painful situations even when I saw an out. When I had the opportunity to escape, I chose to stay. Recognizing bad situations before they happened was always overlooked, giving people the benefit of the doubt. The end result was always harsh and dismissive. I have dated men who sadly enough today I don't even remember their existence. I became cold.

I had never truly fully experienced real love in my adult life because I hadn't been open to it. There have been some that had my best interest at heart without what seemed to be motive. And I rarely have had the feeling of wanting to be in a relationship. However, when I am in one, I am focused, committed and show out with all that I have to offer with no boundaries. Sadly enough what I was giving was never matched, and I gave chances to men who were interested in or choosing me, and me learning to like and love them, for all the wrong reasons.

Men displaying any type of aggression toward me send shockwaves to my system. I become uneasy and my radar goes up. I remember not being able to see the signs of insecurity in someone I was in a relationship with. The first complaint was my attire. He asked if I had shorts on under my skirt, as if I wasn't a grown woman and didn't know how to bend down. He would get tight-lipped if other men were around me or looked at me. I would get the silent treatment as if I had control over that. When it was time to have a talk, he would approach me, punching in his hand while talking. It all escalated to a final blowup of him cursing me out in public due to a misunderstanding.

I witnessed so much violence growing up, even before my tragedy. So it wasn't surprising for me to walk in the opposite direction of a fire to avoid getting burned. The day I was stabbed, I walked right into danger. I had no idea it could get any worse than it did from what I had seen. I say this to say: Today, the escalation of an aggressive act can go from zero to 60 in my mind. I shy away from it quick, shutdown and have walked away from relationships and friendships with only premature signs of it.

I was once told that I am a delicate flower, and in more ways than one, I agree. I demand to be handled with care.

Due to trust and fear issues, I never slept next to a man long enough to get comfortable or to miss someone being in my bed and space. When I experienced it, it was a serious adjustment. I often tossed and turned or slept with one eye open.

Once upon a time, I would sleep with a two-by-four next to my bed and a stun gun. My nightmares would get the best of me when I was in my weakest state. So having this protection next to me seemed to help me sleep. Having a man around in those hours made me feel uneasy because I didn't think they'd ever understand.

I yearned to be comforted and loved, and I pray that the person who sweeps me off my feet will be the one who makes me feel so comfortable, I will look forward to coming home to be wrapped in his arms, feeling safe, with all my issues becoming a distant memory. One who accepts me from the hair on the top of my head down to my toenails, with everything in between. I am prepared to do the same.

It was quite convenient to make time and see men when I could and wanted. At a distance worked best for me as a protective shield.

One day, the Elder of the church I had joined, shared a word with me on relationships. He explained the importance of having a partner. He always had a way with words and it made so much sense. He compared how a couple moved in the world to a workout session at the gym. If you go to the gym and worked out alone, you might not be pushed to your limits, but things would be much different if you had a spotter. We are able to attain more in a workout, and in life, with a partner.

It made so much sense. Understanding the concept of sharing responsibility was not familiar to me. Taking care of self and everything around me was all I knew.

I have had few committed relationships in my life thus far. Although they each ended for different reasons, I am able to pull out the great experiences that I had to add to my lists of needs and wants in my future love. Good friendships came out of all but one.

Either the relationship happened too early on when we were both too young to make lifelong decisions, and needed to venture out into the world and find ourselves, or I was so caught up in my world of issues, that it became too much for the relationship. The attention, consistency, persistence, and sense of humor were all that caught my attention then and were what was necessary. They endured the long drawn-out talks about my situation and still stuck around for the duration. Relationships in those times were my great escapes from the madness I was going through. Again, the friendships that came out of them are truly golden.

Then there were the relationships that were memorable in other ways that turned me off from dating. I hated myself for all that I didn't take the time to get to know before going as far as I did, thinking I had something to do with their behaviors. Being forced to make a decision that goes against my beliefs, but after asking for forgiveness, having the strength to truly walk away with no regrets or looking back. Fool me once, shame on you, fool me twice, can't look to put the blame on no one but myself. Having him out of my life helped me to have no regrets about my decision.
It's all so interesting how I played the role of my mother and him my father, experiencing much of the same issues.

We gravitate toward people with the same characteristics, common interests or need. However, when your issues are similar, how do you help one another to be better? Some people aren't meant to be your everything.

It never mattered the age, the older men I entertained were just as bad in some areas as the younger men. The start of anything new is always so beautiful. There was one that was most memorable because I made more of a conscious effort, considering it would be the first man in my daughter's life after her father. The assertiveness that he showed in his interest and then his approach in asking me to be the woman in his life gave me the feeling that he was grown and knew what he wanted, and it was I. How he went about assuring me and making feel secure, made me feel safe enough to then introduce him to my daughter.

He was consistently around and involved in both our lives. After we had being seeing each other for a while and an unforeseen situation happened with my current apartment, I relocated to move closer to him. I had the usual reservations beforehand, but the move helped the relationship to flourish, giving us more opportunities to spend time together.

Over the next few months, we shared a lot of blended family activities, weekend trips and barbecues. Then, I brought up the idea of having another child in the future. I had had no desire for more children after my bad experiences. But what I had developed with him changed my feelings. I loved how he was so involved in family life, opened to the many activities we had shared together and had been bold enough to approach me and ask for what he wanted. But when I shared my desires with him, the brother told me if I ever got pregnant, I would be getting an abortion because he didn't want any more kids. I threw up in the back of my throat, and at that moment, it was over.

I realized there were things I needed and wanted that differed from him, and walking away was the best thing for me.

Relationships and bonds should be based on shared goals. My church elder preaches that we spend so much time lusting and admiring and staring into each other's eyes, that when we stand side by side, and face forward, we are then able to see if we are going in the same direction when we take our first step together. Your step may be forward and his or hers is to the left or right. The truth is displayed, and relationships end.

They say God does things for a reason and I believe it. I believe that we are given things in HIS time when we will fully appreciate them and understand them. He sends people into our lives to help us recognize things about ourselves for personal growth. Through my encounters with people, I have been able to recognize their purpose afterward and pull out the good.

FRIENDS

The friends in my circle make up those people that God has brought into my life, and life with them has been awesome as well. I am a loner, though I have my moments when I like to be near or surrounded by people. However, I've grown to learn that we make time for what we really want and for whom we really want to be around. For example, it's just a natural feeling to make plans on an impulse alone or with my daughter. But I do my best to spend time or call to catch up with people in my circle.

I meet many daily but I am very selective about who I keep in my circle.

Hanging in large groups of women is not my cup of tea, so I can count on one hand how many sister-girl meets I've been a part of. It's always been easier for me to sit in a male circle. The talk and expectations are different.

Female talks seem more competitive, catty, with high emotions even between friends who are like sisters. Women will dress up in their Sunday best to go hang out with their girlfriends just to prove that they are winning, against each other. They speak of the newest item they've purchased, how much a new bag or outfit cost, where they got their hair done, going in on the specifics of where it was done, who did it and how much it cost. All of the stresses in their lives that warrant a toast. About which I have no desire to speak.

Conversing with men is more laid-back and free flowing. No expectations, less emotions and insightful.

Interestingly, many of the female friends I have, I've met on the job. Unless they were older and posed as a mother figure, the nature of my previous relationships with women were usually brief or drinking alcohol was in the plans.

I am more of a one-on-one type of chick. But recently, I had my first experience of being behind closed doors with another woman daily, her and me. For the first three years at my previous position, I was alone, just the way I liked it. Once Olivia came on board, all of that changed. It's almost as if we are presented with our challenges to become better beings. At first, I didn't think much of Olivia's presence because she would be taking a great deal of work off my plate.

Olivia was a couple of years younger than me, and had her master's degree and a strong sense of self-worth. I was appalled and knew I could use some assistance in those areas. I realized that among my friends, I was the only one to have a bachelor's degree and had never felt motivated or inspired enough to go any further. I realized that there could be a lot to learn from educated women, outside of the cattiness.

As time went on, it became apparent to me that I was more comfortable than I would've imagined. While training her for the position, we would spark conversation about any and everything. She became a trusted, full-of-knowledge woman off whom I would bounce ideas and plans. The much-appreciated advice given helped me in many goals I had set.

Taking a few steps back to regroup and look deeper within of what seems to be obvious to another but not to me, was a focus that has shaped me for the better. She had helped me develop in areas that weren't on the forefront. She had no idea of the mental notes I had been taken. I was so grateful to her and so happy I could reciprocate the favor and help her in a way that was satisfying to both of us, when I was able to get her to the hospital in time to deliver her first baby.

My work life is where I have made the most amazing longtime friendships, tracing back to the age of 14 years old. I have come to meet people from all walks of the world. A minister when I'm in need of prayer, looking to her for advice and nurturing. It is just something about a friendship that is developed with God being the common denominator. Co-workers, where our connection is similar to a smooth takeoff, flight and landing with no turbulence. Down to supervisors and directors who have been great supports.

Ms. Dottie is another good friend. I met her when we were working at a voting poll. How funny life is. She lived in the same area I grew up in and I only saw her in passing. I wasn't scheduled at a voting location and I was assigned to her site, which was right around the corner from my apartment. We spoke of everything under the sun, making it so easy to allow her in. She was very transparent, just like myself, and for that I was grateful. She was old enough to be my mother, but I had always gravitated to older people who were more warm and insightful. She's since moved away, but we have a bond that is built on solid ground and is unbreakable and I am forever grateful for her and I make it a point to let her know.

David, Ray, Steven, Malcolm, and Teddy have been longtime friends. Some going back to when we were 14 years old. I remember my friend Ray had stopped by to hang out with me when I was going through a financial struggle. Once we got to talking and discussing my issues, he dropped the amount of money I needed on the bed without a second word or look, and walked out. When I reached out to return the money, he said, "What money? Stop playing." He is and will always be someone I hold dear, and one day, just one day, he may be in need and I hope to be there to for him as he was for me.

Some played the big brother role and have been consistently near if needed. Most of everything described in this book, they have been there for. Malcolm always teases me and says he has a bill for me from the many times I called and he was my shoulder.

God gives us everything that we need. It is up to me to be open for it and recognize that there is a stronger reason behind it. There are many of us lacking something that we are searching for and your lifeline of help is sometimes right under our nose.

ACCEPTING

With the help of friends and prayer and long talks with myself, I've now reached the point of acceptance. It has been a journey. There were many events that happened about which I questioned the hows and whys. I challenged many believers of God's existence. How do we know heaven or hell will be our next home when we leave this earth? We have a book of stories of our ancestors that describes many things that we experience today called the Bible. Did man write this? Why is it when the pastors give their sermons, they seem to be tailored to your current situation or are ones you can relate to? We often obtain things we wish and hope for. It is said that it is in God's time and not our time. Why is this not by chance, or just being at the right place at the right time? The good seem to die young. Nice guys finish last. Do the people who are wicked and seek to destroy others have a conscious? And why is it, at times, the punishments are not enough and seem to give them more ammunition to do it again and worse the second time around? Is religion a form of discipline or a tactic to keep order in the world, just as stoplights control traffic?

For years, I was so bitter and angry, not understanding the hows and whys of God's movement and why I was chosen to suffer. I was both mentally and emotionally off balance. For instance, how I never felt that my mother's attacker getting a sentence of 25 years to life was enough punishment for what he had done. I felt an eye-for-an-eye would have been justifiable and more comforting to the families that had to cope with the pain he caused. Some say jail is more than enough punishment because it gives killers and rapists time to think about what they have done and hopefully experience some remorse over time. Somehow, that still didn't sit well with me. Animals belong in cages, but when they come out for air, who knows what their mind state will be.

I became a believer in Jesus Christ and our Heavenly Father when I began to develop my own relationship with HIM. It may sound crazy, but in the many hours growing up that I spent in my dark room, I would speak my thoughts out loud and really didn't know if anyone was listening. But through the signs HE has shown me time after time, HE has proven his existence. Again, many can argue it is by chance. However, I am very specific in my prayers and the answers are clear and concise. When I pray, let go and let God, there is a feeling of relief because I trust that it will all work out as it always does, if it is for me. My mind is then at ease and my body becomes relaxed.

I have learned not to cry over spilled milk because it's done and out of my control. I am human, so I do catch feelings when I am expressing my thoughts on an issue or situation. Then when I come down off my emotional high, the solution is to simply "let it go and move on." This statement can often be easier said than done, and you must be ready.
What is for you will be. Whether it is today or next year.

I am not in church every Sunday, but when I do attend, the pastor's message is usually one that is needed and gives me the hope and the fuel I need. There has never been a time that I didn't walk out feeling refreshed and ready to take on the world. The seed that is planted in me gets the water to its soil.

The Sundays I attend church are usually when there is a serious need to be present. No alarm clock is needed. Something inside moves me. I make it a point to get there early for the praise and worship hour. My insides are tickled, massaged then filled with goodness. I am then looking forward to the word of the day that is almost always a message for me.

Music is my "thang." It sets a tone and mood for me. The sweet melody of music fills the air and comforts me. Whether it is R&B and hip-hop, or my favorite, gospel. The oldies but goodies take me to a place in time when things were normal. In my weakest moments, I find my spiritual playlist on iTunes to be very soothing and comforting. It is as if God knows what his child is in need of and HE speaks to me through music. Most artists have the opportunity to share their personal experience through music, art, writing etc., which becomes an outlet and something very therapeutic to which many can also relate.

One of my favorite playlists on my iPod is listed below. While listening to the words of any of the songs below in my time of needing a spiritual touch or healing, a sensitive nerve is touched because tears stream down my face almost immediately. Afterward, I feel renewed.

- Yolanda Adams —albums *Day by Day*, *I Believe*, *Mountain High Valley Low*
- "Church Medley: We've Come This Far By Faith/I Will Trust in the Lord"— Donnie McClurkin
- "Still I Rise" — Yolanda Adams
- "I Want To Say Thank You"— Lisa Page Brooks
- "The Question Is"— The Winans Family
- "Healing"— Kelly Price
- "The Presence of the Lord"— Christ Tabernacle Choir
- "All I Need"— Brian Courtney Wilson
- "Who Would Imagine the King"— Whitney Houston
- "Something About the Name Jesus"— The Rance Allen Group and Kirk Franklin
- "I Believe"— James Fortune & FIYA
- "Take My Life"— Micah Stampley
- "I Need an Angel"— Ruben Studdard
- "I Speak Life"— Donald Lawrence featuring Donnie McClurkin
- "God Favors Me"— Pastor Hezekiah Walker
- "Secret Place," "We Must Praise," "Thank You, Lord"—Amber Bullock
- "A Piece Is Passion" — Juanita Bynum
- "Holiness Is What I Long For" — Donnie McClurkin
- "Now Behold the Lamb"— Kirk Franklin
- "Thankful" — Mary Mary
- "Fragile Heart" from Yolanda Adams' album *Mountain High, Valley Low*
  (This song always brings me to the brink of tears.)
- "I Believe" — James Fortune, Shawn McLemore & Zacardi Cortez
- "I Smile" — Kirk Franklin
- "Stand"— Daryl Coley, Marvin Sapp, Helen Baylor, Maurette Brown-Clark
- "Never Would Have Made It"— Marvin Sapp
- "The Essential"— Yolanda Adams
- " I Am"—Kirk Franklin

Marvin Sapp's "Never Would Have Made It" has always brought me to a place of appreciating all that walked my journey with me. It doesn't matter my emotional state. At times, I am rejoicing in the goodness of being able to recognize how far I have gotten and other times I am just thankful to still be of sound mind with the ability to keep moving despite it all.

Rarely do we know people; until you spend time with them can you see what's really beneath the surface. You may know me, but have no idea who I am. - Unknown

I look much better than what I have been through. - Unknown

I have been told that I have the patience of Job and infinite inner strength. A few years ago, I took the time to read the book of Job and cried because, similarly, he faced many challenges and was stripped of everything. From his family to the assets he acquired over the years to survive, and his faith never wavered. What I witnessed is imprinted in my memory bank. It shaped my thinking and took over my dreams and level of peace. However, deep within the crevice of my soul, I believed that somewhere, somehow better existed. Although I couldn't strongly see the light, I knew the light at the end of the tunnel was near.

My struggles are not in vain. I didn't realize it then, but I truly appreciate the experiences and the will and strength I possessed to have survived and conquered.

For years, looking forward was scary to me. My fears were beyond facing the unknown: How many more hurtful situations will I have to face before I either break and lose my mind, or finally get to a place where I have hurt so much that I grow cold, hardened and heartless? My balance scale was tilted and seemed broken. Will I get to a place in life where hope is restored and my drains will be flushed and circulation within my body can flow normally?

It is human nature to worry and wonder about your next move in life, but it takes the joy out of living. Today, I can happily say that looking back doesn't hurt as it used to. In fact, when I look back and reflect, it gives me hope and strength to deal with current struggles. I often compare pain and hardship from then to now, and realize that my tolerance for pain has increased, which makes my current hardships manageable. The experience is never to be forgotten. However, overtime my pain has begun to fade and it is almost like a distant memory.

My unresolved issues of the past had me stagnated. Constantly looking back blinded me from seeing what was ahead. Negative thinking and a feeling of hopelessness consumed me. I grew to expect a ball to drop when there were moments that should have been celebrated in my life. It was hard to accept the good when the bad was almost always expected and even more easily accepted. Good things happening to me were almost too good to be true.

There were too little breaks in between my hardships and loss. Leaving me feeling defeated and always asking the question of what I had done to deserve such a life. I don't remember ever having an interest in even celebrating a birthday until I turned 21.
I remember describing life as running through the a forest barefoot with the ground being like burning charcoal and the tree branches thorns ripping into my skin as I tried to move them to get a clear view at what was ahead. I had tunnel vision, over analyzing and internalizing every situation and experience I faced.

Now, I've started to realize how valuable I am and how far I've come. Overtime my scale has begun to show signs of not being broken, and today, I learn to take the good with the bad. Curve balls and obstacles are designed to alter your current plans and focus, strengthening and forcing you to make the best decisions and to keep your eye on the prize regardless of circumstances. To teach you something through an experience that will build and shape you into the person you are destined to be.

IN HIS TIME – ANEW

My spiritual walks have kept me. Over the years, I found my way and strength when I attended various churches. The experience was therapeutic. It was a place where people weren't afraid to share a testimony then cry, shout and rejoice. It was quite remarkable and admirable as I wasn't that open.

I had been in church since I was a little girl. But it was forced, as most things seemed to have been in my life. This made it hard to decipher what was necessary. Much of what was taught and preached wasn't absorbed because of my combative attitude. In my teenage years, I met my good friend Sierra and would go to church with her every so often. It was in the neighborhood and convenient. There was never any pressure to attend church, which made it that much more enjoyable. Gave me the freedom I needed.

I met Sierra during junior high school. She became my sister in Christ. We connected on a spiritual level that has never been broken. Her house became a getaway for me. It was close to where I lived, but far enough away from the norm of my situation and life. Just want I needed. Her mother was another mother for whom I held in high regard and respect. She was a woman of God.

Once I moved away from the area, I either found another church to visit or would return to my home church where I was comfortable. I had never committed to any church home at this point. The word commitment has always scared me and I realized most of my involvements were even short and sweet.

Years later, I reconnected with a high schoolmate named Pam and she shared her experiences at her family church. Her having the feeling that she wanted to be there every Sunday and involved in all of the activities made me curious because I had never had that feeling for anything. Most of all, if it led to me wanting to do something like that with my family would be the icing on the cake. I wanted that feeling and made it a point to attend the following Sunday.

The feeling I got from her church was so pleasant and overwhelming, I found myself in church not only on Sundays but also at Bible study on Wednesdays as well. The elder who preached was phenomenal. I was able to understand every sermon and message. Her family embraced me and showed concerned as if I was a part of the family, deeper than just church family. We had a sleepover retreat, dinner in the city and a revival session outside of church and it was all refreshing. A real family!

After months of attending, I decided I was ready to walk the walk, talk the talk and be baptized. I was baptized on Watch Tower night, New Year's Eve 2009. A fresh mind, year and new me. What I didn't know is that as a Christian, there will be more challenges and temptations to face. Being more aware of what is expected of you as a child of God and shaping your lifestyle, mind and heart to be more Christ-like is a challenge, but worth it. The devil becomes mad because he has lost one and is always around to see where he can catch you slipping.

I am far from perfect, but a work in progress.

The beauty of my spirit can solely come from all that I have endured, and I am able to reflect and recognize that my essence comes from the powers of a higher being. The presence of GOD truly lives within me.

HE is the one that I turn to in any situation now, without question. I don't hold God accountable for any painful situation. Instead, I am grateful He has always been there to lift me up. I am learning that pain is a part of life and living.

There is still a great deal of pain that lives within, and when it becomes unbearable, I just say a prayer and ask God for a Heavenly hug. God is funny because on such nights, my mother, Aunt Mira or Grandma Flore usually show their face as if it's a celebration, in familiar settings where laughs and hugs were shared. When I wake the following morning, all of the night-before worries and negative feelings have been replaced with motivation and inspiration to get through another day.

My purpose here on this earth hasn't been found as of yet, but I am getting closer.

The many sermons from the pastors and elders, the inspiration message forwards or social network posts were relatable and comforting. A few that stuck in my mind that allowed me to see that trials and tribulations of life help shapes us for greater life pleasures and to be better beings are shown below:

- *The song "It Is Well With My Soul" was written by a successful Christian lawyer. He had four girls and a wife and the family planned a summer trip to go overseas. Since he had a lot of work to do, he sent his family and decided to follow them later. He heard the news while on the following ship that another ship had capsized and he knew that his family was on it since they mentioned the name of the ship. On his return home, his Law Firm was burned down and the insurance refused*
  to pay, they said, "It was an Act Of God." He had no money to pay for his home
  and no work. Then while sitting and thinking about what's happening to him, being a spiritual person, he wrote a song:

  "Whatever my Lord, you have taught me to say
  It is well, it is well with my soul."

A good attitude will determine your altitude. When you look at your life, career, job or family life, what do you say? Do you praise God? Do you blame the devil? A good attitude toward God makes Him move on your behalf. Just sit down and say, "Today God, it is well with my soul, I am thankful I had a peaceful sleep, I am thankful I am alive with possibilities. I am thankful I have a roof over me. I am thankful I have a job. I am thankful that I have Family and Friends. Above all, I am thankful that I have the Lord Jesus Christ on my side. "Be blessed and do not be envious or shocked when others are prospering because you do not know what they have been through to get where they are (tests, trials and tribulation), so thank God for what you have. "Little is much when God is in it."

This story was similar to the book and life of Job as well as my own.

We tend to look to GOD when we are in need, instead of praying until something happens. Building a relationship with HIM outside of your needs brings an infinite lifetime of, and at times unseen, blessings.

Try it by just thanking him for the basic needs and things you currently have.

Only God can turn a Mess into a Message, a Test into a Testimony, a Trial into a Triumph and a Victim into a Victory. -Unknown

I have learned to pull out the message in every unpleasant situation I have been in once it has been surpassed. This allows me to receive the message God is sending me. Many have told me that God speaks to them if they listen hard enough. I have never been able to hear anything. However, through signs, as I always pray and ask for, I am able to get that message.

In Bible study, one Wednesday night, Elder spoke on our scars of life. He explained how God heals us. The bandages applied on our bruises not only helps in the healing but makes us that much stronger and resilient. Bandages and scars make us who we are and different from one another. Elder knew my walk of life and experiences. So using me as a demonstration allowed for me to begin to understand the way in which God operates. HE is always there to help in your healing if you would just look to Him. Also, HE helps to protect you from harm.

From the moment I wake up, stress and worry filled my mind. Less now than before after recognizing that this is not of God. My immediately response to an issue is not to call anyone to consult or get opinions but to sort and plan my approach. I made it point to try my many options but when I am at a lost and have no other choices, I then turn to God. The answer is revealed much sooner than the time I spent solving the problem. I have learned to take a moment and breathe and consult with my father first for obvious clues. From my past experience, I have had the privilege of seeing how he moves, I can attest to this post I recently read:

> *"Don't Worry. God is never blind to your tears, never deaf to your prayers and never silent to your pain. He sees, He hears and He will deliver."* - *Unknown*

I refrain from watching worldly news as much as I can because it deepened my depression and heightens my hopeless feelings of life.

One of my favorite shows is *Law and Order*. Interestingly it captures my attention for hours. It's almost an obsession. I haven't fully come to terms as to the difference between the worldly news and this show because although *Law and Order* is a television show, it's based on true stories aired on the news. During the day and evening when I watch *Law and Order*, afterwards before bed, I would turn to one of my favorite cartoons to change my thought process and emotions. These decreased my chances of having a nightmare.

They say every second someone is birthed into the world, someone dies. If this were an experiment, than it would make sense because the results are controlled. The reality of it all is the level of violence that is reported every day in either the news or in the newspapers is disturbing. Whether near or far, I can easily sympathize with the families hurt. It is almost as if I'm reliving a moment. For example, my hope and faith was strengthened after local news reported a story on an emergency plane crash landing and all survived:

January 2009, a plane was struck by a flock of birds and was forced to land in the East River. The captain made the decision to make an emergency landing and successfully got all the passengers to safety. There was a man that spoke out sharing his experience. He mentioned being so scared and was just trying to keep it together. An announcement was made to let all women and children off first. Order, respect and calmness in the storm. It touched me.

That day marked a new beginning for me and all who were part of this experience. The fear that takes over when hearing the unexpected, preparing for the worst, but hoping for the best, frigid cold waters and all survived. Amazing!!!!!

The message to me from Elder the Sunday before that happened was: Because of my faithfulness, a blessing is coming this WEEK. Although this miracle didn't directly affect my family, or me, it had a personal, internal effect on me. Eternal joy. My increased feeling to live and believe was more than one could ask for. I took that as the blessing. I love success stories. They make me smile and just look up.

Another moment where my faith was strengthened was a few days before Mother's Day. I was low on cash because I had just gone back to work after having been temping for six months. I usually treated my daughter to IHOP for breakfast to celebrate her making me a mother. I could not afford to go out, let alone buy any fun foods to celebrate. I had a bank account that I had not used in months because it was not my primary account. I grabbed the mail out of the box as usual, and as I walked up my six flight I pondered a plan. When I got in I plopped down on the sofa and did something I did not normally do. I opened the bank statement; something that I had not done in months because I didn't think there had been any activity. To my surprise, $1350 was sitting in the account. I was shocked. The bank said it was the interest. I had the bank look at the history and bank officials reiterated that the amount was due from monthly input of interest deposits. To have sat down in that moment when I was worrying and wondering and in need, and getting a prompt to do something I usually never did, was simply Him guiding me to my blessing.

FINAL THOUGHTS AND PURPOSE

Life is a gift that we are blessed with. It is yours to do with what suits you as we are all different and don't share the same common interest or goals. It is like a card game. We all are dealt a hand that is different from one another. How well you play depends on how well you know the game. This requires paying attention, learning the game and strategizing.

There aren't any road maps, dictionaries or encyclopedias to surviving, succeeding or raising children. Some of us are lucky to be given information and the tools needed to survive from the first people we learn to love and trust, our parents. Others merely learn from experiencing the unknown and witnessing the outcome. Learning from your own experiences becomes your road map, dictionary and encyclopedia.

Some of us are born into turmoil that becomes life-long if change doesn't happen. There are long lines of generational hurt, abuse and neglect in some families that continue this cycle. They don't know any better and they pass down the same information and behaviors to their offspring. We do not have to be products of our environment. Be courageous and step out anew. When we know better, we do better.

Most parents define wanting to provide a life for their child that they never had as simply giving them more monetary items. They don't realize that exposure to the unknown for greater knowledge for a better future is key. Someone has to break the cycle.

There are people who haven't experienced suffering, but have the worst attitudes and the most complaints. They are their own worst enemy and hindrance.

Having a bad hand dealt to me and having to play it like the most expert poker player has been challenging, but there are many rewards to fill the need for peace and comfort. Pain is inevitable, but doesn't last forever. I was ashamed of the cloth that I was cut from, thus didn't appreciate the person I had become. I used to think all of my imperfections and issues were so rare, that they would keep others away. Never could I imagine marriage or children. Damaged goods were how I saw myself.

I went back and forth for years about writing and publishing a book. After facing my unresolved grief and other issues caused by post-traumatic stress disorder, I have developed the courage. It is still a work in progress. From as early as I can remember in my elementary and junior high years, I would write in my journals. By day, I was like the sun, shining bright with few signs of dysfunction. By night, in all my depression and gloominess, my pen and paper was in hand. This allowed me to release the negative energy, expressing my deepest emotions and thoughts. As time went on, I thought of collecting all that I had written and compiling them along with current experiences. But I needed to truly understand my purpose. What would be my goal for sharing my life story and experience with the world? I have had people say, "You are good, because I would never do such a thing." For years, I second-guessed the book idea, pushing it to the side many times.

But being in a better space in my life, truly accepting all that has happened in my life, it is worth sharing in order to be a message for another. "Each one, teach one" is something that should be the way of the world. The gift of getting older is to get wiser through experiences. Leaders of the world play a huge role in the lives of the generations that follow.

During childhood, we often have little control over our lives, and many things can happen that can influence us into our adulthoods. It is up to you to grab hold of your life to be a better you.

Feelings of shame and embarrassment used to overcome me when I thought of my life. I felt as if I were the only sane one, the only one striving to make a difference. Then I began to think that I was the odd ball. I blended in well in other parts of my life, but it felt as if I didn't belong in the family that raised me.

Having a better understanding of self has allowed me to embrace and appreciate my past as that is what has made me the person I love today. Changing something could alter a characteristic or unique quality. Knowing that no matter what you do you cannot change a person and accepting that person has allowed the embarrassment and shameful feelings to vanish.

At times, I think of how I go out of my way to give my daughter everything that I was not fortunate enough to have. Creating better opportunities for her to get further than I did to have a better future. I don't want her to feel my pain and struggle completely, but going through struggles made me resilient and successful. So, now that she is old enough to understand, I plan to expose her to struggle by taking her to homeless shelters to help feed the needy. I want her to have a greater appreciation for what she has.

They say only the strong survive. When life threw me lemons, I made the best damn fresh squeezed lemonade.

Success doesn't accurately measure one's intelligence or maturity. Some people have roads or platforms provided to them. Successfully achieving a sense peace by gaining a better understanding of and finding an acceptance of self has meant more to my life than any amount of money or degree achieved.

Writing this book has been very therapeutic and has provided another level of healing by challenging me to uncover things that hindered and kept me mentally trapped and bound.
I found my thoughts and ideas tumbling out after many days in bed in pajamas with my laptop. What was once viewed as a dark space has evolved. The room is still my favorite comfort zone. However, it's now as bright as the sun on a summer day. It's funny how the season has changed in my comfort zone now that clarity and acceptance exist.

I recently had an experience where I was forced to tell my story to a group of people who had no interest in me; it was rather painful. It broke me down and weakened me. I felt vulnerable and fragile. But after a few days of feeling that way, I came back to myself. I felt different. The experience had made me that much stronger. I realized it had been a stepping-stone to get to this point of sharing my story with the world.

This book is an heirloom for my daughter, a foundation of strength. My mother had to suffer, while I watched for God to work on and through me to be the rock needed for her and a blessing to another. Assisting me in breaking the generational cycle paved a way for Star to be a more proud, better, stronger, more powerful her. No greater gift to inherit.

THE END

Thank you for your purchase of this read that is dear to me. This is a true story of my journey thus far. I am still a work in progress, healing and learning but I am on my way. With God's grace, I will continue to heal and live out my destiny.

GOAL

To Motivate and Inspire.

OBJECTIVE

To express the importance of speaking up and out. Harboring ill feelings and keeping painful secrets are toxic and bad for your health. Seeking help, if needed, is healthy and perfectly normal. Your past does not dictate the results of your future. Release for a better quality of life.

PROMOTING

Good Mental, Physical and Emotional Health.

Please visit my website and leave a comment or review.

www.adiamondintherough.co

Lakesha Nicole Baker

91299666R00126

Made in the USA
Columbia, SC
19 March 2018